More

THAN A

PURPOSE

MARSHALL DAVIS

More
THAN A
PURPOSE

AN EVANGELICAL RESPONSE TO RICK WARREN
AND THE MEGACHURCH MOVEMENT

A Division of WINEPRESS PUBLISHING

Pleasant Word (a division of WinePress Publishing, PO Box 428, Enumclaw, WA 98022) functions only as book publisher. As such, the ultimate design, content, editorial accuracy, and views expressed or implied in this work are those of the author.

ISBN 1-4141-0663-7
Library of Congress Catalog Card Number: 2006900114

DEDICATION

This book is dedicated
to my wife, Jude, my lifelong companion
and
the love of my life,
who prayed this book to completion.

TABLE OF CONTENTS

Acknowledgments

I would like to thank the First Baptist Church of Rochester, Pennsylvania, for giving me a three-month sabbatical leave to write this book. I hope that the fruits of this time away from my pastoral duties are deemed worthy of the investment.

I would also like to thank Bill Marshall and the Marshall Center of Georgetown College, Georgetown, Kentucky, for the use of their flat at Regent's Park College, Oxford University, England, where I spent part of my sabbatical leave. Being able to view American Christianity from the other side of the pond helped to refine this book.

I would like to thank my wife, Jude Davis, who read, discussed, prayed over, and critiqued every page, and Glenn Vander Wagen who proofread and commented on the final manuscript. His suggestions resulted in many changes that made the book better.

Finally, I thank my Lord Jesus Christ. By his grace I am saved, and with my life I seek to glorify him. Thirty years ago I vowed that if he would permit me to write a book that any financial gain from it would return to him. I now keep that vow. All profits from this volume will return to the work of his church. I pray that this book may help his earthly bride to glorify him with authentic worship and faithful service.

INTRODUCTION

After reading Rick Warren's *The Purpose-Driven Life,* I felt like singing the chorus of Sugarland's country hit, *Something More.*[1] I thought to myself, "There has to be more than this!" The book had enthralled every Christian I knew. "You have got to read it!" they insisted whenever I sheepishly admitted I hadn't gotten around to purchasing a copy. Churches in our neighborhood began sprouting banners declaring their involvement in the "Forty Days of Purpose." I felt like the disciple Thomas who had missed Jesus' Easter visit. Just so I would not be the only pastor on earth who had not read this primer on the Christian life, I picked one up at Wal-Mart. That experience itself was disturbing; I am not used to buying my theology off a rack next to bawdy romance novels.

By the time I acquired my copy it already came embossed with a gold star on the cover declaring it to be a #1 Bestseller. The back of the book gushed endorsements by preachers and authors I admired like Billy and Franklin Graham, Max Lucado, and Lee Strobel. The Graham team urged me from the book jacket, "Make sure you're not missing the point of your life—read this book! *The Purpose-Driven Life* will guide you to greatness...." Anticipating greatness I began to read, expecting a Spirit-empowered presentation of the gospel for the twenty-first century that would transform my ministry in ways I could not yet imagine. Instead I got indigestion.

I didn't know exactly why my spiritual digestive system was upset. To be honest, it all seemed rather mundane. Why were people so excited about the book? It is insightful in places, but not profound. The five purposes (worship, fellowship, discipleship, ministry, evangelism) are standard fare in any freshman Ministry 101 class. Warren even gave an altar call in the book, something that should have warmed my evangelical heart. But even his evangelistic invitation left me unsettled. What was wrong with me? Why did I feel no compulsion to jump into the Saddleback model of ministry? I read the book a second time to see what I had missed. It was then I realized that it was not me, but the book that was missing something.

I love homemade pancakes: not made from a pre-made mix out of a cardboard box, but a stack from scratch. I will use only 100 percent pure maple syrup; no Mrs. Buttersworth for me. One Saturday night my wife cooked a batch of her superb pancakes on the griddle and placed the golden beauties before me. Something didn't look quite right, but I poured on the "New Hampshire gold" and dug in. I could tell immediately that something was wrong. My wife noticed my silence, and asked if everything was OK. I replied, "Is this your regular recipe?" "Sure. I always make them exactly the same." After a few more minutes of silence, she remarked, "I might have forgotten to put in the baking powder."

Something was missing. The pancakes looked different; they were not the light fluffy creations I remembered. They also tasted different, but I could not have told you exactly what was wrong. Something is missing from *The Purpose-Driven Life*. Many people notice, but don't know exactly what is wrong, and they conclude it must just be them. The truth is that there is a lot missing from *The Purpose-Driven Life*. This realization led me to investigate the history and the philosophy behind the *Purpose-Driven* model of church growth. After much study, thought, and prayer, I have concluded that *The Purpose-Driven Life* is the proverbial canary in the coalmine. If corrective action is not taken, it forebodes dangers for the future of evangelical Christianity.

It is not that Saddleback Valley Community Church is a California cult and Rick Warren a Hawaiian-shirted Jim Jones. It is just that vital elements are missing from the Saddleback view of Christian faith and practice. Since the book is designed for seekers, many readers may not be able to tell the difference between the *Purpose-Driven* gospel and historic Christianity. But for me, reading Warren's books is like eating Bisquick pancakes with maple-flavored corn syrup. I grew up in New England eating homemade pancakes and listening to the sound of maple sap dripping into buckets. For Yankees like me, anything less than "Grade A Light Amber" still warm from the sap house will not do. Rick Warren's bestseller doesn't go deep enough or far enough. This book is for those who want more, who want to go deeper and further than *The Purpose-Driven Life* can take you.

Rick Warren likes to use the Southern California metaphor of surfing to describe his *Purpose-Driven* model of ministry. In fact he entitles the introduction of *The Purpose-Driven Church* "Surfing Spiritual Waves." He sees the Holy Spirit making waves, and he wants to teach pastors to ride the wave of God's blessing.[2] There are waves all right. In fact, it is downright stormy in the American spiritual seascape these days. Warren is certainly riding the waves like a Californian surfer. But much of the time he is riding the waves of American cultural trends rather than the waves of the Holy Spirit.

If Rick Warren were just some ordinary Baptist pastor in California, I could chalk it up to West Coast craziness. But Warren is gaining a worldwide following. George Mair's laudatory biography of Warren, *A Life With a Purpose*, has as its subtitle, "Rick Warren, the Most Inspiring Pastor of our Time." In the book he calls Warren "a religious legend," "the most admired Protestant preacher in America," and "America's most important Protestant religious leader." He considers Warren's impact on Christianity to have global significance.[3]

Warren is part of a movement that is changing the face of evangelical Christianity. He has branded it as nothing less than a "Second Reformation." "The first Reformation was about belief; this one's going to be about behavior," said Warren…"The first one was about creeds; this one's going to be about our deeds. The first one divided the church; this time it will unify the church."[4] He sees himself wearing the mantle of a reformer, a new Martin Luther, nailing his Five Purposes to the door of evangelicalism. On April 17, 2005, speaking before a crowd of 30,000 members and attendees at the church's 25th anniversary celebration in Angel Stadium, Warren said: "My hope is for a new reformation in the church and a new spiritual awakening throughout the world."

This megachurch movement cannot be ignored by those who think Warren is driving the church astray. Like Paul confronting Peter in Antioch when he was "not straightforward about the truth of the gospel," evangelicals need to "withstand him to his face" (Galatians 2:14,11). Warren's *Purpose-Driven* gospel is not a Christian reformation. It is not a restoration of the biblical gospel that has been some-how clouded under centuries of church tradition. It is a reinterpretation of the gospel that compromises its truth.

I do not question Warren's love for our Lord, his sincer-ity, or his passion to reach the lost. He fully believes that he is preaching the same old-time religion his father preached, just presenting it in a new way. In fact his form of Christian-ity is a twenty-first century incarnation of the old mainline Protestant liberalism. John MacArthur says that evangelical-ism has changed significantly in recent decades. The change is so dramatic that what is now called evangelicalism should more accurately be labeled neo-orthodoxy.[5] Chris Accardy calls Warren's gospel "Neo-Liberal Evangelicalism."[6]

Purpose-Driven Christianity still remains Christian...for the moment. But it is an abridged form of Christianity that is sliding into dangerous territory. Many Christian elements have been omitted, and many worldly elements have been imported. It is a hybrid that in the next sowing may lose its distinctly evangelical nature. "Winds of doctrinal com-promise are beginning to stir," says MacArthur.[7] These are the winds that are pushing the waves that Rick Warren is surfing.

The purpose of this volume is to examine the strengths and weaknesses of Rick Warren's *The Purpose-Driven Life* and to offer an alternative vision of the Christian life that will reclaim the evangelical heritage and essentials. This is not an exposé of a cult; it is an exhortation to a brother. My goal is not to tear down Warren or his ministry, but to build up the body of Christ. To do that, truth must be told. Warren observes that most pastors do not have someone who will be honest enough with them to speak the pain-ful truth.[8] Warren has made it difficult for him to hear dissenting opinions because he has surrounded himself with "court prophets" who will only speak what he wants to hear. Those who do not share his approach to church growth are asked to leave his congregation.[9]

This book is my attempt to tell the truth. Whether it will be painful to him, I do not know. It is painful to me. To him and his followers I will probably be seen as nothing more than a troublesome mosquito to be swatted. In *The Purpose-Driven Church* Warren casually dismisses anyone who challenges his theological orthodoxy as not being his "target audience."[10] Therefore I doubt I will cause any pain in Orange County, California, but I hope to shed some light that will help readers discover that there is more to evangelical Christianity than what Warren is presenting.

CHAPTER ONE

IT'S NOT ABOUT YOU...OR IS IT?

The first chapter of *The Purpose-Driven Life* opens with the words: "It's not about you."[1] Rick Warren then explains the difference between his book and self-help books, saying that self-help books are self-centered and geared to self-actualization, whereas his book is different. He emphatically states that his is not a self-help book.[2] At Warren's Saddleback Church, his bestseller is jokingly referred to as the "anti-self-help book." Is this true? Is *The Purpose-Driven Life* truly a different genre than the self-improvement books that fill whole sections of Barnes & Noble?

The very first words of the book are found on the dedication page. Before the Table of Contents, several pages before Warren tells us it is not about us, he says, "This book is dedicated to you."[3] That statement sets the tone for the volume. In spite of the protestations by Warren and his supporters, *The Purpose-Driven Life* is nothing more than a Christian variation on the self-help theme. The book's preface tells us the purpose of the book is "to reduce your stress, simplify your decisions, increase your satisfaction, and most important, prepare you for eternity."[4] This is the language of self-help with a spiritual twist.

Warren's world is a man-centered universe. Although God plays an important supporting role, man is the center—or at least one of the centers. Warren's universe is like one of the distant solar systems revealed by the Hubble telescope that has two suns. There are two foci in Warren's spiritual system around which everything else revolves: God and man. Whereas he repeatedly declares that God is the only true focus, it seems like the *Purpose-Driven* universe revolves around us.

He quotes a geneticist in Day Two, saying that the whole cosmos is designed with man as its purpose.[5] On the next page he quotes a poem by Russell Kelfer, who tells us that we are the special focus of God's attention. Nearly half of the lines begin with the word "you."[6] According to Warren the purpose of the church is to meet *your* needs. God instituted the church to help *you* with *your* problems, strengthen *your* faith, discover *your* talents, and find *your* mission in life.[7]

This is Your Life

In spite of statements to the contrary, *The Purpose-Driven Life* is about you. It is all about your life and how you can make it better. On Day Three he lists the five benefits of living the purpose-driven life. *The Purpose-Driven Life* "gives meaning to your life," "simplifies your life," "focuses your life," "motivates your life," and "prepares you for eternity."[8] Warren reminds us occasionally of his original premise that life is not about us but about God.[9] But God, it appears, exists for our purposes as well. God's purpose is to fulfill us in every way.

If Warren's book is not exactly a self-help book, it certainly is a self-fulfillment book. Warren has built up his church on meeting the "felt-needs" of seekers, and *The Purpose-Driven Life* drives that central point home. If you adopt the *Purpose-Driven* model for your life, then you will have what no self-help book could ever deliver–a life in which God fulfills your every need. Warren has tapped into one of the major themes of American culture, and that is why he is so successful. George Barna, the astute observer of American culture, writes: "The Bible instructs us to approach God with fear and trembling, befitting our awe at his majesty and love, focusing on who he is, what he has done, and what He expects of us; the culture encourages us to treat God as an equity partner focused on our personal development."[10]

Where did this approach come from? To understand Rick Warren you have to explore his roots. Warren says that to understand a person's theology—whether Martin Luther's, John Calvin's or his own—you have to understand the historical context of the person's life.[11] Biography is the forge in which theology is formed. You can't understand *Purpose-Driven* theology or methodology until you understand something of Warren's life and background.

Warren Family Ties

Rick Warren comes from a strong line of Baptist preachers. He proudly traces his Baptist pedigree back four generations.[12] He traces his spiritual roots to his great-grandfather, who was converted by the great nineteenth-century evangelist Charles Spurgeon at his London Metropolitan Tabernacle. The Warren ancestor later came to America as a circuit-riding preacher.[13] Both his father and his father-in-law were pastors. It is undoubtedly this Baptist heritage that keeps him faithful to the Southern Baptist denomination when most megachurch pastors choose to abandon denominational ties.

In 1973 when Warren was a college student, he drove 350 miles to hear W. A. Criswell, the well-known pastor of what was then the largest Baptist church in America, the First Baptist Church of Dallas. He considers Criswell the greatest twentieth century American pastor.[14] As Warren was shaking Criswell's hand after the service, the aged and influential preacher felt compelled by God to lay his hands on Warren and give him a blessing. Like Elijah conferring his mantle on his disciple Elisha, Criswell prayed that a double portion of God's Spirit might rest upon the young student and that he might pastor a congregation twice the size of the Dallas congregation.[15] Warren understands this prophecy to be fulfilled in Saddleback Valley Community Church. He asked Criswell to write the foreword to *The Purpose-Driven Church*.

The man who had the most influence in his life was Rick's father, Jimmy Warren, Sr. The elder Warren was a traveling evangelist with the Southern Baptist Convention in Northern California. In time he became the director of missions for the Yokayo Association, which meant that he was a pastor to pastors. The importance of this type of ministry made an impression on Rick. Today he sees one of his ministries as training and equipping other pastors. His popular website, Pastors.com, is a testament to his belief in this important equipping ministry.

The most profound ministry-shaping event of Rick Warren's life was the death of his father. In *The Purpose-Driven Life*, he powerfully relates the story of his father's dying words. Jimmy Warren had terminal cancer and was in a state of delirium during his final days. Struggling to get out of the hospital bed, he kept crying out, "Got to save one more for Jesus! Got to save one more for Jesus! Got to save one more for Jesus!" He repeated that phrase over a hundred times. Warren relates the scene. "As I sat by his bed with tears flowing down my cheeks, I bowed my head to thank God for my dad's faith. At that moment Dad reached out and placed his frail hand on my head and said, as if commissioning me, 'Save one more for Jesus! Save one more for Jesus!'" Rick Warren has made that command the theme of his life.[16]

In the movie, *Knute Rockne: All American*, the character played by Ronald Reagan says from his deathbed, "Tell 'em to go out there with all they got and win just one for the Gipper." To understand the ministry of Rick Warren, you have to understand the "Gipper factor." Rick Warren is trying to fulfill his father's dying words. He wants to "Save one more for Jesus!" He is going to do anything it takes to save as many as he possibly can. Such a passion is deserving of great praise. Personally I take off my shoes in the presence of any man who makes that the dominant theme of his life. It is this zeal for the lost that has made Rick Warren's church so successful. It is this passion that he tries to communicate to others through his books and ministry.

This commitment to evangelism has made Rick Warren a successful pastor. His desire to win more and more, faster and faster, for Jesus has also led him to adopt questionable philosophies and methodologies. Many believe it has led him to compromise the gospel in order to win more converts. Warren discovered that if he changed the presentation of the message, more people would listen and respond positively. This came about through the influence of a new understanding of evangelism that became popular in the twentieth century.

Donald McGavran and the Church Growth Movement

Rick Warren first came into contact with the thought of Donald McGavran in 1974 when Warren was a student missionary to Japan. He happened to run across an article about the Indian-born missionary. He remembers sitting and reading the article, having no idea at the time that this would impact the direction of his ministry in such a dramatic way.[17]

Donald McGavran is the father of the modern Church Growth Movement. The son of missionaries, and later himself a missionary to India, McGavran studied what made churches grow. Later he came to Fuller Theological Seminary in Pasadena, California, and founded the *Fuller School of World Mission* in 1965. In 1973 his friend, Win Arn, founded the *Institute for American Church Growth*, where McGavran served as the chairman of the board of directors from 1974 until his death in 1995. Together they co-authored the first book on American church growth, *How to Grow a Church*. Many other books followed. As a young pastor fresh out of seminary, I was captivated by the books of McGavran and Arn. *Ten Steps For Church Growth* by McGavran and Arn became my second bible as I led my congregation to understand the sociological principles that would enable our small church to become super-sized.

The Church Growth Movement applied sociological research and scientific principles to the numerical growth of American congregations. The central teaching was that a church grew if it obeyed certain empirically observed rules that govern congregational growth. One particularly con-troversial rule was the "homogeneity principle," which said that churches only grow by reaching out to the same type of people that are already in the congregation. This laid open the authors to the charge of racism and segregation, charges that they repeatedly denied. The Church Growth Movement taught that churches grow by understanding and utilizing sociological principles of how social organizations grow. It is a science and applies to all organizations. Any church can grow if it obeys the rules and principles of growth.

The Church Growth Movement is the underlying philosophy of *The Purpose-Driven Church*. Warren openly admits that the day he read the McGavran article was a life-changing event. He sensed a divine presence directing him to dedicate the rest of his life to studying the principles that produce church growth.[18] Warren has even adopted the controversial "homogeneity principle" and identified his target audience as Saddleback Sam, a white, well-educated male, married to Saddleback Samantha with two kids, Steve and Sally. He is in his early thirties or early forties, likes contemporary pop and country music, with a cell phone at his ear, a pager on his belt, and is skeptical of "organized religion."[19]

After returning from Japan, the seminary student, Warren, took up this study at Southwestern Baptist Theological Seminary. He did an independent study of the one hundred largest churches in the United States in order to discover why they grew so large. Rick Warren has now become the model of the success of church-growth principles. He is the champion of the Church Growth Movement.[20]

The Church Growth Movement is primarily the application of scientifically discovered principles to the church. These principles are not unique to Christian organizations. They can be successfully applied to any organization—secular or religious, Christian or non-Christian. It is this attitude that is epitomized in the *Purpose-Driven* seminars. Mormons and New Age religions are welcomed into the seminars, and they successfully employ the principles of church growth taught there. *USA Today* reported "Warren's pastor-training programs welcome Catholics, Methodists, Mormons, Jews, and ordained women." In the interview, Warren said, "I'm not going to get into a debate over the non-essentials. I won't try to change other denominations. Why be divisive?"[21]

The *Purpose-Driven* model is rooted in the scientific study of organizational growth. It attempts to blend biblical truths and sociological laws, but sociology is the driving force. The Bible is used to buttress the truths discovered in scientific surveys. Never are any biblical truths contrary to church growth voiced. The *Purpose-Driven* church has never seen congregational growth it didn't like. What is important is that the church grows. Why it grows and how it grows are not critically examined. It is assumed that if a church is growing, then God is causing the growth.

The fact is that Jesus intentionally drove away crowds of people who were following him simply to have their needs met. Jesus said, "Most assuredly, I say to you, you seek Me, not because you saw the signs, but because you ate of the loaves and were filled" (John 6:26). He goes on to give them what the disciples called a "hard saying" about who he really is and what it takes to follow him. Jesus explained the only valid cause of church growth was the call of God, saying, "'Therefore I have said to you that no one can come to Me unless it has been granted to him by My Father.' From that time many of His disciples went back and walked with Him no more"(John 6:65-66). James White says that Jesus was the founder of the Church Shrinkage Movement![22]

Norman Vincent Peale

Rick Warren may be the most famous figure in the Church Growth Movement at the present time, but he is only the latest representative in a line of preachers that stretch back to Norman Vincent Peale. Peale gave birth to the movement that birthed Warren. [23] Warren's biographer calls Peale a "New Age preacher" and the originator of the self-help movement, which is the foundation of the Church Growth Movement. Peale linked psychology and religion, thereby creating a therapeutic religion that became the message of megachurches.[24]

Peale wrote forty-one books, but is best known for *The Power of Positive Thinking*. In this book he taught that you could change your life by changing your attitude. The fundamental problem of modern man, according to Peale, is negative thinking, especially fear and self-doubt. The solution is simple: train yourself to think positively. By prayer, meditation and the repetition of inspiring thoughts and Bible verses, Peale says, one can develop a positive mindset that results in a happy and fulfilled life. For Peale, Christianity is fundamentally a change of attitude that results in physical, mental and spiritual well-being. The essentials of the gospel of Jesus Christ are missing from Peale's work and replaced with a "mixture of Christ and Freud—Christianity and psychiatry."[25] Warren adopts Peale's concept of Christianity as "a mental shift" when he redefines the biblical idea of repentance according to Peale's philosophy. Repentance is no longer the biblical idea of turning away from sin; it is simply a change of mind. Warren says that we repent whenever we modify our way of thinking to conform to God's way of thinking.[26]

Peale got many of his ideas from the occult teacher Florence Scovel Shinn in her book, *The Game of Life and How to Play It*. Many clergy accused Peale of plagiarism by lifting phrases out of her writings as well as borrowing her ideas. Most evangelical writers find Peale's psychological reinterpretation of Christianity and his occult connection as evidence that he has strayed from the historic Christian gospel. Warren's biographer finds nothing wrong with Peale's approach and applauds the connection between Peale and Warren. The two share the same merging of psychology and religion, the same desire to reach the average person, and the same downplaying of biblical theology in favor of self-improvement techniques. Mair proudly exclaims, "Saddleback distinctly bears the stamp of Reverend Norman Vincent Peale."[27]

Robert Schuller

If Peale is the grandfather of the *Purpose-Driven* philosophy, Robert Schuller is the father. Saddleback Church is built on the same foundation as the Crystal Cathedral. Schuller was the first megachurch pastor with a national reputation. He began as a Dutch Reformed pastor in Chicago, knocking on doors and trying to build up his congregation. Nothing seemed to work. His sermons were dull, and the people stayed away in droves. Desperate to find the secret to attracting a crowd, he began reading everything he could find about motivation and communication. Two books changed his life: *How to Win Friends and Influence People* by Dale Carnegie, and Norman Vincent Peale's *The Power of Positive Thinking*. Schuller's study of these two books led to a transformation in the way he understood his vocation. No longer did he see his task as preaching to the lost to bring them to Christ. He now understood his job as "positive preaching" for the purpose of lifting people's spirits.[28]

From that time on, his ministry began to flourish. He moved to Orange County, California, and held worship services in a drive-in theatre, which he rented for $10 a Sunday. He preached from the tarpaper roof of the concession stand to his flock of automobiles. While his church was still small, Schuller invited Norman Vincent Peale to preach, and the famous preacher accepted the invitation. This cemented the relationship between the two men, and imprinted the Peale philosophy on the Schuller message. Schuller recounts that from then on he preached the Peale gospel. The only difference was in the name. Instead of "positive thinking," Schuller called it "possibility thinking."[29] This theatre congregation grew into the Garden Grove Community Church, the Crystal Cathedral, and the nationwide television ministry "Hour of Power." In 1969 Schuller began the *Robert Schuller Institute for Successful Church Leadership.* Among its early alumni was the future megachurch pastor Bill Hybels of the Willow Creek Community Church.

This institute had a powerful effect on Rick Warren's life. Robert Schuller describes how Warren came to his institute for pastors "time after time." Warren's wife Kay said, "When we came to the institute we were blown away."[30] In an article about Warren in *Christianity Today*, Tim Stafford writes: "During his last year in seminary, he and Kay drove west to visit Robert Schuller's Institute for Church Growth. 'We had a very stony ride out to the conference,' she says, 'because such nontraditional ministry scared her to death. Schuller, though, won them over. Kay Warren admits that Schuller "had a profound influence on Rick."[31]

Indeed, the spiritual teaching of Robert Schuller's self-esteem movement has been adopted by Rick Warren and built into the core of *The Purpose-Driven Life.* The positive thinking reformation of Schuller, announced in his 1982 book *Self Esteem: The New Reformation,* is being continued by the New Reformation of Rick Warren. Schuller's central concept is that if you change the way you think, you will change your life. Warren agrees: "To change your life, you must change the way you think. Behind everything you do is a thought. Every behavior is motivated by a belief, and every action is prompted by an attitude."[32] Warren even took his central concept of purpose from Schuller's book. "God chooses us to serve his purpose. 'You did not choose me, but I chose you.' Our self-esteem is rooted in our divine call. God's dream for our life and work gives purpose and pride to our life."[33]

A close relationship between Robert Schuller and Rick Warren continued for many years. Warren spoke at Schuller's *Institute for Successful Church Leadership* on several occasions during the 1980s. He and his wife, Kay, appeared at the Crystal Cathedral in 1991. Warren served on the council of Schuller's *Churches Uniting in Global Mission.* Schuller continues to endorse Rick Warren's ministry and *The Purpose-Driven Life.*

But in 1991 Warren had a falling out with Schuller over his invitation to Stephen Covey to speak at the Crystal Cathedral. Covey is a devout Mormon who has publicly ridiculed evangelicals and the Christian gospel. In protest Warren resigned from Schuller's organization and has since refused Schuller's repeated invitations to have Warren speak at Schuller's institute. This break between Schuller and Warren is well-documented in Richard Abane's book, *Rick Warren and the Purpose That Drives Him.*[34] It is clear that Warren and Schuller have parted ways. But Schuller's legacy remains in the teachings and methodology of *The Purpose-Driven Life.*

The Itchy & Scratchy Show

At the heart of the *Purpose-Driven* model is the meeting of "felt needs." For Warren, a church must discover what people feel that they need, and give it to them. Robert Schuller uses the slogan, "Find a need and fill it. Find a hurt and heal it." A more accurate slogan might be, "Find an itch and scratch it!" Warren calls this the "seeker-sensitive" approach. Everything Warren does is driven by the felt needs of his target audience. He discovers what they want, and he delivers, and they swarm back to get more of the same.

This is a therapeutic gospel with its roots in pop psychology. *The Purpose-Driven Life* is peppered with the language of psychological illness and recovery. He calls sins faults and failures.[35] The problem of man is that he feels insignificant. This can be remedied by adopting a new understanding of life that proves our worth and gives us a greater sense of satisfaction.[36] Warren says that Gideon's problem was low self-esteem and a feeling of insecurity.[37] The apostle Paul had a problem with depression, we are told, which was resolved by sharing his feelings through his epistles as a form of writing therapy.[38] Warren embraces the recovery model, saying that we are only as sick as our secrets. His solution is an evangelical eight-step recovery program called *Celebrate Recovery* based on the eight beatitudes of Jesus (to distinguish it from the secular twelve step programs).[39]

The Seeker-Sensitive Jesus

Warren finds the seeker-sensitive approach in the New Testament. The apostle Paul was an advocate of the approach, according to Warren. Although he admits that Paul did not use the term "seeker-sensitive," he sees the apostle as the pioneer of the concept. [40] Warren goes so far as to say that seeker-sensitive worship is a biblical command in Paul's' writings.[41] For Rick Warren the supreme model of seeker-sensitivity is the ministry of Jesus. He says that Jesus regularly used the felt needs of his audience as an opportunity for evangelism.[42] Warren has even incorporated the "felt needs" concept into the bylaws of Saddleback church. The purpose of Saddleback Church is to meet the needs of the people of the Saddleback Valley.[43]

How does a church discover which of the many human "felt needs" to meet? Warren's answer is to survey the community. He congratulates one church that found that the number-one need of people in their community was "potty training for preschoolers." They designed their evangelism program around this need and justified it by Proverbs 22:6. "Train a child in the way he should go."[44] For some reason I have a hard time picturing Jesus calling the little children to him and then instructing their parents on toddler toilet techniques.

This focus on felt needs is not just a hook to get people in the door to hear the gospel preached from the pulpit. It also determines the message delivered from the pulpit. Warren says that most pastors are asking the wrong question. Instead of asking the Lord what they should be preaching on Sunday, pastors should be asking their "audience" what it is they want to hear! The needs of the people are, according to Warren, the voice of God instructing the preacher about the content of the message.[45]

Traditionally the preacher's Monday morning question was: "What is it that God wants me to preach this Sunday?" Events in the lives of his church members were important, but not the determining factor. According to Warren, the preacher should not ask what message should be preached, but what human need should be met. Preaching no longer finds its primary inspiration in God's Word, but in man's needs. It is no longer what God desires of us, but what we desire of God. Warren says we need less "ought to" sermons and more "how-to" sermons.[46] After the needs are identified, Warren brings in the Bible to find Scripture texts to meet the needs. But this approach means that the portions of the Bible that don't address human needs will never be preached from a *Purpose-Driven* pulpit.

God does meet human needs. But the gospel doesn't start with our needs nor end there. The gospel begins with God, ends with God, and God is everywhere in between. Fulfillment of our needs is the overflow of a God-centered life that does not consider its own needs. Furthermore, it is not the "felt needs" of man that are important, but the real needs of man. What a person *feels* he needs might not be what he *really* needs. God is not in the business of coddling our feelings, but in conforming our lives to the image of his Son (Romans 8:29).

Warren has received criticism from evangelicals for his self-fulfillment approach to the gospel. Speaking to a group of Southern Baptists, R.C. Sproul said, "Often the modern Gospel is presented as meeting felt needs while faith in Christ alone is scuttled...The Gospel is not about purpose for your life. The Gospel is not about making you feel good. In the first instance, the Gospel is about who Jesus is and what He did."[47] In regard to Warren's attempt to kick-start a new reformation he says, "The message that is often preached is not the full-orbed biblical Gospel that God uses to bring about genuine revival and reformation. Authentic reformation and revival will come only when the Gospel is preached in its biblical purity and fullness...A reformation is nothing we can generate on our own."[48]

Not surprisingly, Warren does not see himself as compromising the gospel in any way. On the contrary he considers himself as the champion of the seeker-sensitive gospel of Jesus. Warren paints himself as the heroic trailblazer dodging arrows in an attempt to open up new territory for the gospel of Christ. He says his critics are the same old "religious establishment" that has always opposed the gospel. He likens them to the scribes and Pharisees of the first century who ruthlessly criticized Jesus' "sinner-sensitive ministry." Warren labels his opponents as "isolationists" who are being "extremely judgmental." Their critiques are "unfair characterizations made out of ignorance."

Warren sees himself as a martyr for the cause of Christ. Comparing himself to John Wycliffe, Warren writes.

"Translating the truth into contemporary terms is always dangerous business. Remember, they burned Wycliffe at the stake for doing it."[49] As I write this, I am on sabbatical leave at Oxford University, where Wycliffe was a leading theologian. The Oxford dons will be surprised to learn that Wycliffe was martyred. History tells us that he died peacefully at his home of a stroke on New Year's Eve, 1384. Thirty years after his death, the Roman Catholic Church condemned him for heresy. Thirteen years later his bones were exhumed, burned, and his ashes scattered. Likely Warren is confusing Wycliffe with William Tyndale, who was burned at the stake 150 years later.

Warren's critics accuse him of cheapening the gospel and selling out to consumerism, but Warren replies that it is a "theological fact" that God reveals himself according to human needs.[50] Is this true? Did Jesus have a need-based ministry? Sometimes Jesus used the healing of human infirmities or the satisfying of human hunger as opportunities to present the gospel. But more often Jesus asked people to forsake their needs for the sake of the gospel. One rich young man felt the need for financial security, a theme often affirmed by evangelicals today. Jesus told him to sell everything he had and give it to the poor and come follow him. That man left "sorrowful" because Jesus would not accommodate his requirements to the man's lifestyle (Luke 18:22-23).

On another occasion Jesus met a seeker who expressed his desire to follow him. The only thing he asked of Jesus was a decent place to sleep at the end of the day. Jesus' promise was that he would have "nowhere to lay his head." Another seeker felt the responsibility to care for his father until he died. Surely Jesus could accommodate such a loving motive. Jesus replied, "Let the dead bury their own dead, but you go and preach the kingdom of God." Another felt it was only right to say goodbye to his family first. Jesus responds, "No one, having put his hand to the plow, and looking back, is fit for the kingdom of God" (Luke 9:57-62).

Rather than pandering to seekers' felt needs, Jesus urges his hearers to abandon their own desires and follow him. All the needs of our lives, felt or real, need to be abandoned at the feet of Jesus. "Whoever seeks to save his life will lose it, and whoever loses his life will preserve it" (**Luke 17:33**). "He who loves his life will lose it, and he who hates his life in this world will keep it for eternal life" (**John 12:25**). Rather than seek the fulfillment of our needs, Jesus teaches us to deny ourselves. "If anyone desires to come after Me, let him deny himself, and take up his cross, and follow Me" (Matthew 16:24).

One time Jesus had been very successful in drawing a crowd. "Now great multitudes went with Him. And He turned and said to them, 'If anyone comes to Me and does not hate his father and mother, wife and children, brothers and sisters, yes, and his own life also, he cannot be My disciple. And whoever does not bear his cross and come after Me cannot be My disciple. ... So likewise, whoever of you does not forsake all that he has cannot be My disciple'" (Luke 14:25-27,33). In the face of numerical success Jesus preached a seeker-offensive message that drove away the crowds and left only the ones chosen by his Father. Clearly there is more to the message and ministry of Jesus than meeting felt needs!

The Sovereignty of Human Needs

What are we to make of the preeminence of "felt needs" in Warren's understanding of the church's ministry? For one thing it assumes that people know what they need. It presupposes that what a person *feels* he needs is what he *truly* needs. In the practice of the megachurches, the expressed desires of potential worshipers are assumed to be legitimate needs that need to be met by the church. This unexamined presupposition is the weakness of the user-friendly church. We live in a psychologized society that has fabricated all sorts of "needs" and given them a public hearing in daytime talk shows. The deeper, unarticulated needs of the soul are ignored. The deepest need of man is for God. The essential problem of man is his attempt to have his needs met apart from God. Felt needs are a diversionary tactic of the enemy of the human soul.

Man does not know what he wants. What he feels he needs is perhaps the worst indication of what he really needs. Warren talks a lot about listening to your heart and following your heart as an indicator of the will of God.[51] The heart is the source of the needs that Warren is trying to meet. But according to Scripture, the heart is unreliable in discerning what we really need. The prophet Jeremiah said: "The heart is deceitful above all things, and desperately wicked: who can know it?" (Jeremiah 17:9). You hear the advice a lot today: "Follow your heart." That is terrible advice. Do not follow your heart; follow what is dear to the heart of God. Follow what God says in his Word.

The Bible does not tell us to follow our hearts. It tells us to guard our hearts. "Above all else, guard your heart, for it affects everything you do" (Proverbs 4:23, New Living Translation). If we follow our hearts, it will get us into deep trouble. Our hearts do not know what we really need. We need to educate and train our hearts by meditation on the Word of God, the discipline of private prayer, and the company of godly men and women. The heart is by nature corrupt, and its felt needs are corrupt. It sows corruption and reaps corruption. The heart is like a spoiled child that demands immediate satisfaction without regard to what is right or wrong or the consequences of the action. It will lead us away from God.

If a church follows the "felt needs" of the unconverted, it will succeed only in scratching the itches of the flesh and will do nothing to heal the sickness of the soul. The apostle Paul warns preachers against scratching itches. He tells the young preacher Timothy to preach from the Word and not preach to needs. "Preach the word! Be ready in season and out of season. Convince, rebuke, exhort, with all longsuffering and teaching. For the time will come when they will not endure sound doctrine, but according to their own desires, because they have itching ears, they will heap up for themselves teachers; and they will turn their ears away from the truth, and be turned aside to fables" (2 Timothy 4:2-4). The Christian preacher is not to give the people what they want; he is to give them what God's Word says they truly need.

If you feed people's heart-felt needs, your church will grow. There is no doubt about that. The Church Growth Movement is correct in that assessment. If you are good at meeting needs, then your church will grow like Saddleback Church has grown. It is a surefire formula for numerical success. But you will have gained the applause of the world and lost your soul. The focus of the church must be the will of God and not numerical growth.

You will not find in the apostle Paul's letters any instruction to the churches to give the people of Corinth or Thessalonica what they want. He did not instruct Timothy to distribute a questionnaire to the people of Ephesus to find out what they were looking for in a religion. He did not instruct physician Luke to do research on the physical needs of the people of Asia, nor did he ask Mark to conduct a demographic study of Rome. He told them to faithfully proclaim the gospel of Christ.

Warren's focus on "felt needs" reveals the deep theological problem with the seeker-sensitive approach. It abandons the sovereignty of God for the sovereignty of man. This approach has infiltrated the seminaries. Seminarians are no longer trained to proclaim the demands of God to a rebellious people. They are taught to lure people into their churches by accommodating their desires. People's needs have become sovereign, and the sovereignty of God is ignored.

The roots of the *Purpose-Driven* concept are in man-centered psychology rather than God-centered theology. The driving force is the well-being of human beings instead of the will of God. Science drives the church, while theology is relegated to the infant carrier in the back seat. The Dr. Philesque infatuation with psychological health has made Christianity into a therapy for hurting hearts instead of salvation for lost souls.

The Dead Preachers Society

In *The Purpose-Driven Life,* the key to the true Christian life is commitment. Before the reader embarks on the forty-day journey of purpose, he is asked to sign his name to a commitment. It is called a covenant, which in the Bible is the most serious obligation one can make. In the *Purpose-Driven* covenant, the reader agrees to commit to spending forty days seeking God's purpose for his life. [52] This is the beginning of a program that makes the concept of commitment the heart of the Christian life. If your life is without purpose, then make a commitment to discover the purpose of your life, and it will be done for you.

In *The Purpose-Driven Life,* salvation is accomplished through commitment to God. In Warren's scheme, salvation does not begin with the sovereign act of God bringing to life a dead soul, what the Bible calls regeneration. Instead it begins in a commitment that a living soul makes "with God's help." But the Bible says, "But God, who is rich in mercy, because of His great love with which He loved us, even when we were dead in trespasses, made us alive together with Christ (by grace you have been saved)" (Ephesians 2:4-5). The difference between these two understandings of salvation is the difference between Christianity as a rebirth or a "mental shift."

Warren sees the problem of empty pews as a lack of commitment. He observes that people in today's society no longer know what commitment means. People make and break serious commitments with a casual attitude.[53] He sees that as the problem with the traditional church. The difference between a church member and merely a church attender is commitment, he says. Warren urges Christians to commit themselves completely to Christ and to the church.[54] Rick Warren's goal is to get people to sincerely and wholeheartedly give themselves to the service of the Lord.

Not only is salvation a commitment, spiritual growth is also a commitment. It is the end result of a sincere desire to grow, followed by a decision to grow, and a persistent effort to grow.[55] Our commitments shape our lives and determine our future. Commitments define who we are. We become our commitments.[56] Warren's understanding of salvation hinges on commitment—directing enough psychological energy to accomplish one's spiritual goals. This is exactly what the self-help books preach.

In the 1989 film, *Dead Poet's Society,* Robin Williams plays an English teacher in a private boys school who inspires his students to commit themselves to lives of excellence. In an early scene he takes his charges out into the hallway to see trophy cases filled with old photographs of boys long dead. He impresses upon them the reality of their own mortality, and whispers to them, "Carpe Diem. Seize the day, boys. Make your lives extraordinary." *The Purpose-Driven Church* is the Christian equivalent of the *Dead Poet's Society*. Rick Warren whispers into the ears of his readers, "Seize the day. Commit yourselves to the purposes of God. Make your lives extraordinary." This was the message of liberal Protestant preachers in the nineteenth century, who, having abandoned the gospel of grace, replaced it with a strident call to moral living. We might call this the *Dead Preacher's Society*.

Commitment to purpose gives your life meaning in Warren's gospel. "Nothing precedes purpose."[57] Because *The Purpose-Driven Life* has its roots in psychology, the problem with man is defined in psychological terms. The solution is a psychological reprogramming of your life. What is needed is a psychological adjustment, a mental "extreme makeover." The mental picture of our lives needs to be replaced. We need an image transplant.

My Life as a Car

A British radio comedy series, entitled "My Life as a Car," traced a man's life from adolescence to late middle age using his automobiles as metaphors for his progress in life. Rick Warren's metaphor for the Christian life could be given the same title. For Warren, a Christian is driven like an automobile. Warren consciously employs this mechanical understanding of his metaphor, likening the Bible to an automobile owner's manual.[58] Traditional metaphors, such as disciples following a Master, or a sheep following a Shepherd, are insufficient. We are now motor vehicles, and the Bible is our operating manual.

Rick Warren wants to change your "life metaphor." The idea of a life metaphor is crucial to Rick Warren's book. He asks his readers to imagine their lives in terms of a mental picture. He says that this image is our life metaphor. It is our view of life, whether or not we have consciously chosen it. It is our self-understanding of how our lives work.[59] He gives examples of such metaphors. Common metaphors include life as a minefield, a roller coaster, a circus, and a journey. Life is like a carousel with ups and downs. It is like a game of cards; you have to play the hand you're dealt. Others see life as a dance or a symphony.[60] Whether the image is spoken or unspoken, it shapes our lives and determines our destinies. A life metaphor is a powerful unconscious force that determines our values, our expectations, our goals, and our priorities.[61]

Warren believes that most people are operating from a "faulty life metaphor."[62] He wants to change your outdated and ineffective life metaphor, that is change your understanding of the Christian life. For Warren the most spiritually powerful and successful life metaphor is to be "driven." What does this metaphor say about Warren's view of the gospel? Is this metaphor in keeping with the biblical understanding of the spiritual life?

Driving Lessons

The word "driven" can have many connotations. After giving seven different definitions for the word "drive," Webster's Revised Unabridged Dictionary says: "Drive, in all its senses, implies forcible or violent action. It is the reverse of to lead. To drive a body is to move it by applying a force behind; to lead is to cause to move by applying the force before, or in front."[63] The word "driven" is used in a variety of ways in everyday speech. A screw is driven by a screwdriver. A nail is driven into a piece of wood by a hammer. A golf ball is driven down the fairway by a club.

To be driven is often to be the object of violent assault. Military defenders drive away attackers. In football the ball is driven down the field. In computer jargon a printer or a mouse needs software called a "driver" to tell it what to do. Cowboys go on a "cattle drive" as they herd their stock off to the slaughterhouse. Cars have a drive shaft. All types of machinery are driven by some power source, whether that is a steam engine or Star Trek *Enterprise's* "warp drive." Is this the best metaphor for understanding how God relates to his people?

Though the connotations of the word "drive" are aggressive, Warren generally uses the concept of being driven in the sense of popular psychology. The word is commonly used to describe the "Type A" personality. If a person has lots of directed energy, whether in business or sports, it is said that he is driven. Entrepreneurs have an inner drive to succeed. Olympic athletes are driven to excel. Politicians are driven to win. It is commonly accepted in our society that to reach the top in any profession one has to have a single-minded determination to work hard and persevere through obstacles to reach the goal. This inspirational "possibility thinking" is the core of the spiritual teaching of Robert Schuller's self-esteem movement and Rick Warren's *Purpose-Driven Life*. To be "Purpose-Driven" is to be motivated to succeed in the Christian life.

This idea is seeker-sensitive and user-friendly. Those unfamiliar with religious terminology can easily understand this view of life. People who have been encouraged by motivational speakers like Tony Robbins to "believe in themselves" and "awaken the giant within" would have no difficulty understanding and accepting Rick Warren's metaphor. Warren wants his readers to excel in the spiritual life the same way that they have been encouraged to excel in other areas of life. The only way people know to excel is to be totally committed, almost to the point of obsession—to be possessed by a power or cause bigger than themselves. All they need is a trainer to inspire them and a guidebook to direct them on the journey to spiritual success. In Rick Warren and his *Purpose-Driven Life* they have found both.

What Would Jesus Drive?

The concept of being driven by the purposes of God is foreign to the Scriptures. The word "drive" or "driven" is used forty-two times in the New Testament.[64] Never is it used of Christians being driven by God or the purposes of God. Usually the word "driven" is used of evil spirits. Demons drive a person, and the Spirit of God drives demons out of people.[65] Most of the time the word is used of impersonal forces, such as boats being driven by a storm or a snake driven out of a fire. Once love is the driving force, when John says, "Perfect love drives out fear."[66]

There are a few occasions where people are driven. Jesus drove the moneychangers out of the temple. God drove the nations out of the land of Canaan. A few times the word refers to believers being driven. Jesus is driven out of Nazareth. The apostles were driven away by persecution. Once it is used in a metaphorical sense of the Corinthians driving Paul to make a fool of himself.[67] In fact the only time the word "driven" is used in a positive sense about Christians is when Jesus says he will never drive a Christian! "All the Father gives me will come to me, and whoever comes to me I will never drive away."[68] Never is the word driven used of God directing his people according to his purposes!

When we examine the Old Testament we find exactly the same use of the word as in the New Testament.[69] The majority of the times it is used to describe pagan nations being driven out of the land of Canaan.[70] The second most frequent use of the word is to refer to the Hebrews being driven out of Egypt or Canaan.[71] The rest of the time the word is to describe animals, chariots, or slaves. People are driven from their homes by enemies. Spears and tent pegs are driven, as when Jael drove a tent peg into Sisera's head![72] Nebuchadnezzar was "driven away from people." Adam and Eve were driven from the Garden of Eden. Their son Cain was "driven from the ground" and from the presence of the Lord.

There are no instances of the words "drive" or "driven" being used in the way that Rick Warren employs the words. Never does God drive his people according to his purposes for them. When God drives them in the Old Testament, it is to drive them away in judgment and punishment. This is exactly the opposite of how Warren uses the term. The God of the Bible never drives his people to fulfill his purpose for their lives. Rick Warren's metaphor of a "Purpose-Driven life" is not a biblical concept. It is foreign to the biblical worldview and Christian theology.

The Islamification Of Christianity

Not only is the concept of being driven by God unbiblical; Rick Warren compounds the problem by making the metaphor impersonal. The hallmark of evangelical Christianity is having a personal relationship with a personal God. But instead of speaking of a *Spirit-driven* life or a *Christ-driven* church, Warren opts for *purpose* as the driving force. In place of a person, Warren has placed a purpose.

In the wake of the terrorist attacks of September 11, 2001, I participated in a series of radio discussions on a local radio show. One of the guests was a Muslim college professor who was also an imam at a Pittsburgh mosque. In the course of the conversations, this moderate Sunni Muslim from Egypt said, "The Muslim finds the meaning and purpose of his life in observing the five pillars of Islam." [73] He went on to describe these five pillars as profession of faith, prayer, almsgiving, fasting, and worship. As I listened to this devout Muslim describe his understanding of his religion, visions of Warren danced in my head. This knowledgeable Muslim had a *Purpose-Driven* life!

Islam is religion with an impersonal and distant deity. The Muslim does not have a personal relationship with Allah. He is Allah's servant. The only way he relates to Allah is by submitting himself to Allah's five-fold purpose for human life. The Muslim is driven by the five purposes of Allah. In an eerily similar way, Rick Warren emphasizes the concept of Christians as "servants" of God fulfilling the five-fold purposes of God.[74]

An image that dominates Warren's understanding of Christian commitment is surrender. In his section on worship, Warren defines *Purpose-Driven* worship as "surrender," which he equates with the term "submission."[75] He says that accepting Jesus as Lord is surrender. Consecration is surrender. Taking up your cross and following Jesus is surrender. Many of the traditional terms for Christian discipleship can be summed up, according to Warren, with the word surrender.[76] Warren devotes a whole chapter to this idea. In the section entitled, "What It means to Surrender," he says that obedience is just another word for surrender.[77] He describes Jesus as the supreme example of what it means to surrender to God.[78] He is likely unaware that this is also how Muslims describe Jesus! For the adherents of Islam, Jesus was an exemplary Muslim.

Linking surrender closely to his understanding of conversion, he says that the Paul's conversion on the Damascus Road was an experience of surrender.[79] Surrender may start at conversion, but it is an ongoing process of submitting to the will of God.[80] He finishes the chapter by saying that the practice of Christianity is nothing more than being a slave of Jesus. He endorses the commitment made by Bill Bright, founder of *Campus Crusade For Christ,* who signed his name to a document that identified him as a slave of Jesus.[81] This same powerful metaphor is a controlling image for Rick Warren's understanding of what it means to be a Christian.

The words surrender, submission and submit, are seldom used in the New Testament, and almost never used in describing the Christian's relationship to God. Almost exclusively they are used to urge human beings to submit to human authority, either of the family, the slave master, or the state. But submission is the central concept of Islam. The word "islam" literally means submission. A "muslim" is literally "one who submits or surrenders" to the will of Allah.

This is not to say that the ideas of surrender or submission are entirely absent from the Bible and unfit for use in the church. Quite the contrary! It is very helpful as one chord in the song of salvation. Any Baptist who has given his life to Christ while the organ played the gospel hymn, "I Surrender All," knows the power of that image. It is a legitimate biblical concept. But it is not the governing metaphor for understanding the Christian life. It is the overpowering dominance of this metaphor in Warren's writings that is the problem.

His understanding of the Christian's relationship to God is distorted. According to Jesus our love for God is the central and controlling theme. Jesus calls love of God the first and greatest commandment. The two commands to love the Lord and love our neighbor sum up our obligation to God. Yet in *The Purpose-Driven Life*, love takes a back seat to surrender. Whereas love is the dominant note of Christianity, submission is the driving force of Islam—and *The Purpose-Driven Life*.

Islam is the fastest growing religion in America and western nations. This is because its understanding of life meets a need in the human psyche—the same need that Rick Warren is meeting! What we find in *The Purpose-Driven Life* is the Islamification of Christianity. In the place of a personal encounter with a personal God, we are offered obedient submission to the five pillars of *Purpose-Driven* religion.

"It is a fearful thing to fall into the hands of the living God" (Hebrews 10:31). That is why so many religions, including many forms of Christianity, attempt to push God away to a safe distance. In God's place, people insert intermediaries. In the early Christian centuries, Gnosticism filled the gap with "eons" and lesser deities, including the Old Testament Creator, which they understood as different than the New Testament Father of Jesus. Roman Catholicism elevated the Virgin Mary to a position of intermediary between man and Christ, who himself was the mediator between God and man. God drifts into the distant heavens. Warren has placed the *purposes* of God between the *person* of God and us.

Warren's vision of living for the purposes of God is an improvement over living according to our own selfish purposes. Now we are to allow God to use us for his purposes rather than our using God for our purposes.[82] The attraction of Warren's gospel is its call to selflessness and discipline in an age of self-indulgence. That is also the attraction of radical Islam to young men like John Walker, the "American Taliban," who was brought up in an ego-coddling American home. But a *Purpose-Driven* life is a far cry from a vibrant, living, loving, personal relationship with Jesus Christ.

From Spurgeon to Springsteen

Rick Warren has a burning desire to save the lost for Jesus. It is his "felt need." In the American religious climate of tolerance, this evangelistic zeal is commendable. The origin of this fervor comes from his family heritage. It was planted in the soul of his great-grandfather by the great evangelist Charles Spurgeon. It was transmitted from father to son, and was conferred to Rick through the deathbed commission of his father. It is a modern example of the godly heritage of the young preacher Timothy. "I call to remembrance the genuine faith that is in you, which dwelt first in your grandmother Lois and your mother Eunice, and I am persuaded is in you also. Therefore I remind you to stir up the gift of God which is in you through the laying on of my hands" (2 Timothy 1:5-6). The apostle told the young preacher to "do the work of an evangelist" (2 Timothy 4:5). That is what Rick Warren has tried to do. Rick Warren comes from a line of Baptist evangelists who knew and preached the gospel.

But the gospel itself became diluted along the way by intermingling with worldly influences. Udo Middelmann, the president of the Francis A. Schaeffer Foundation, calls it "lemonade with too much water."[83] You can still taste the gospel, but it will not satisfy the thirst of the soul. Warren meant to repackage the gospel to reach a new generation, but somewhere along the way the contents of the package leaked out. First the strategies of Donald McGavran and the Church Growth Movement placed the focus on universal principles discovered by sociological research. Then came the tremendous influence of the "positive thinking" of Norman Vincent Peale and the "possibility thinking" of Robert Schuller. This introduced the psychological dimension into Warren's gospel. From here Warren made "felt needs" the determining factor in the ministry and message of the church.

The message of the grace of God to lost sinners became a therapeutic message for hurting hearts. Bruce Springsteen sings that everyone has a hungry heart. Rick Warren has set out to meet the hunger with a designer gospel tailored to fulfill every need of the human heart. The path to spiritual fulfillment, according to Warren, is to get an extreme makeover in forty days, through the study of *The Purpose-Driven Life*. By the end of the book, your life is redefined as submission to a five-part program of divine purpose. Great-grandfather Warren would not recognize the gospel preached at Saddleback Church.

CHAPTER TWO

DOCTRINE FOR DUMMIES

Is *The Purpose-Driven Life* genuinely Christian? Does Rick Warren teach the historic evangelical understanding of how we are saved through Jesus Christ? Those are the most important questions we can ask about his book. If the *Purpose-Driven* gospel is solidly biblical and orthodox in its theology, then all other questions are of secondary importance. If Warren's book clearly presents the Christian gospel, then any disagreement about his style or tactics is nothing more than a family squabble. Then as Christian brothers and sisters, we can sincerely give him our blessing and "agree to disagree" on some nonessentials. After all, Jesus said, "He who is not against us is on our side" (Mark 9:40).

On the other hand, Jesus also said, "He who is not with Me is against Me" (Matthew 12:30). If the message of *The Purpose-Driven Life* deviates significantly from the essential elements of the gospel, then we are dealing with an evangelical counterfeit, which is leading millions of readers to place their trust in a false promise of salvation. The apostle Paul opposed false apostles directly, saying, "There are some who trouble you and want to pervert the gospel of Christ. But even if we, or an angel from heaven, preach any other gospel to you than what we have preached to you, let him be accursed" (Galatians 1:7-8). One of Warren's critics says that Rick Warren is such a false apostle, saying, "Rick Warren is in the process of leading the Church astray."[1]

Warren considers himself to be authentically Christian. Warren's friend and former colleague, Richard Abanes, agrees, calling Warren "a biblically sound Christian."[2] Warren attributes any criticism of his theology to pastors jealous of his success.[3] He acknowledges that there are some churches "that have grown large with faulty theology, shallow commitment and worldly gimmicks," but he says that is not true of his church.[4] In his opinion Saddleback has been unfairly lumped with these other churches because of similarity in size. When critics accuse his sermons of being shallow, he replies that he is not shallow, he is "strategic." Under the surface is a "hard-core biblical message."[5]

Is the Warren gospel a "hard-core biblical message" or is it a mixture of "faulty theology, shallow commitment and worldly gimmicks?" Warren obviously takes the accusations of fellow evangelicals to heart. As a preemptive strike, he subtitled his first book, "Growth Without Compromising Your Message & Mission." He is sensitive to the suggestion that he is compromising the gospel. He repeatedly interrupts *The Purpose-Driven Church* to answer the charges of his critics, but his responses are always the same: deny the accusations and accuse his accusers of impure motives. He never seriously addresses the allegation that he has compromised the message of the gospel in order to make it acceptable to the widest possible audience.

There is a third possibility. Perhaps the truth is between the two extremes. It is possible that we should not paint Warren in white and black, but in colorful splotches like his Hawaiian shirts. Rick Warren may be neither hero nor heretic, neither apostle nor apostate, but just an imperfect pastor trying to further the gospel and grow his congregation. And he has made some serious mistakes along the way. Warren sees himself as a pioneer exploring uncharted territory. Life on the frontier has always involved danger; the spiritual frontier involves theological dangers. Warren walks close to the line of orthodoxy and undoubtedly steps over it at times, more by theological sins of omission than commission. At other times the winds of the world seem to blow him off course. Theologically, it is his carelessness in doctrinal matters that make him most vulnerable to criticism.

The Denigration of Doctrine

For Rick Warren, theology is of secondary importance. In his books, he repeatedly belittles the role of doctrine. He remarks in his chapter on Scripture that the Bible is not just a doctrinal guidebook.[6] That is true. But it is not *less* than a guidebook for doctrine. Second Timothy 3:16 says, "All Scripture is given by inspiration of God, and is profitable for *doctrine*, for reproof, for correction, for instruction in righteousness." Doctrine comes first in the apostle's list! Warren says, "Christianity is not a religion or a philosophy, but a relationship and a lifestyle."[7] That is not true. Christianity is a religion and a philosophy, as well as a relationship and a lifestyle. Christianity has a theology at its core. Warren quotes a modern translation of James 2:24 "We please God by what we do and not only by what we believe,"[8] but he does not balance the passage with Paul's statement that we are saved by faith alone, and not by works (Ephesians 2:8-9).

Warren says that when we die and stand before God that our Judge will not ask us about our religious background or our doctrine. He says that the only thing that matters to God is whether we accepted Jesus Christ as Lord and Savior.[9] This is only half true. You cannot have a saving relationship with Jesus if there is not an accurate understanding of Jesus. Saving faith has theological content. A Christ without content is not the Savior, but rather a theological fiction.

Warren says that it is our love for each other, and not our doctrine, which is important.[10] Over and over again, Warren puts up "doctrinal beliefs" as the straw man knocked down in favor of relational aspects of Christianity. While reading through *The Purpose-Driven Life* you get the definite impression that doctrine is unimportant, unessential, and seemingly unnecessary for salvation. Os Guinness observes that this is typical of the megachurch movement:

> The megachurches' disdain for theology and the seminaries is particularly striking. Anyone receiving a dime for every negative reference to theology would soon be a millionaire. Theology is said to be cerebral, theoretical, wordy, divisive, specialized, remote—an obviously unwelcome intruder to the Holy Family of the spiritual, the relational, and the practical.[11]

Warren goes so far as to say that theological truth can be irrelevant to the task of preaching. He says that what determines the subject of his preaching is not God's Word or the Holy Spirit, but the interests of the audience. He concedes that truthfulness is not unimportant, but not all truths are important enough to preach. Something can be true but irrelevant.[12] Instead Warren preaches what he calls "how-to sermons" filled with practical suggestions and biblical principles for living. He never seems to get around to preaching any theology that does not have immediate application to everyday problems.

Warren prefers not to preach theological sermons because theology does not draw the crowds. He says that if you start quoting theologians you will lose the attention of your audience.[13] He observes that those who proclaim truth do not get much attention today because people are not looking for truth. People value tolerance, but cannot tolerate truth. They are not looking for what is true, but what will bring them some degree of relief.[14] Consequently this is what Warren gives them. Recent polls reveal that 75 percent of people do not go to church to discover truth but to improve their lives. This is what Saddleback Church attempts to deliver.[15] Theology is irrelevant to church growth.

Unity is another important element in Warren's understanding of what it takes to grow a church. He always chooses unity over theology; he never lets doctrinal differences divide his church.[16] When he lists the type of "disputable matters" that cause divisions and conflict in a church, interpretation of Scripture is on the list. He adds that if Christians would only concentrate on love and the purposes of God, then harmony will always result.[17] Love unites, doctrine divides. True to his baby-boomer focus, he holds to the Beatles' philosophy that all we need is love.[18]

The crooning of the Beatle John is a far cry from the theology of the apostle Paul. Paul sees divisions in a more balanced way. Divisions can be the result of carnality. "For where there are envy, strife, and divisions among you, are you not carnal and behaving like mere men?" (1 Corinthians 3:3). But doctrinal divisions can also be part of the process of discerning truth from error. "I hear that there are divisions among you, and in part I believe it. For there must also be factions among you, that those who are approved may be recognized among you" (1 Corinthians 11:18-19). But for Warren, doctrinal disputes are not a testing of truth but a distraction from the main purposes of the church.

The denigration of theology in the life of a megachurch is demonstrated in the doctrinal statement of Saddleback Church. The church's website has a page entitled "What We Believe." It lists the *Purpose-Driven* beliefs. Saddleback's doctrinal statement consists of eleven sentences, each covering one area of theology:

- God is bigger and better and closer than we can imagine.
- The Bible is God's perfect guidebook for living.
- Jesus is God showing himself to us.
- Through His Holy Spirit, God lives in and through us now.
- Nothing in creation "just happened." God made it all.
- Grace is the only way to have a relationship with God.
- Faith is the only way to grow in our relationship with God.
- God has allowed evil to provide us with a choice, God can bring good even out of evil events and God promises victory over evil to those who choose him.
- Heaven and hell are real places. Death is a beginning, not the end.
- The church is to serve people like Jesus served people.
- Jesus is coming again.[19]

This is Doctrine for Dummies. Douglas Webster calls it "sound bite theology."[20] It is Christianity for the theologically challenged. It is so vague that it means almost nothing and excludes almost no one. A Mormon, a Moonie, and a Jehovah's Witness could all sign their names to the Saddleback creed, then join hands and sing, "We are One in the Spirit." Warren says he wants to concentrate on what unites Christians, not what divides them. He paraphrases Ephesians 4:4-6 and says that we are all one body. We share the same Lord, hope, purpose, faith, baptism, love, salvation, and future. These commonalities far outweigh our individual differences. He urges believers to focus on the positive and downplay the negative.[21] What he means is: downplay doctrine and concentrate on relationships.

Warrenite theology is "gospel lite": tastes great, less filling. One reviewer writes: "*The Purpose-Driven Life* is Christianity for grade-schoolers: the style is elementary, the sentences short, the print large, the chapters brief, the theology shallow, the structure overly simplified. For those seeking a spiritual feast in *The Purpose-Driven Life*, leave the fork at home—a straw is all you'll need."[22]

For those who desire more than breast milk in their theological diet, you can follow the link at the bottom of the "What We Believe" web page for a more complete statement of Saddleback theology.[23] When you study this longer document, you can see more clearly the nature of the theological deficiencies of *Purpose-Driven* theology.

Warren is a Southern Baptist. In *The Purpose-Driven Church* he confesses that he is unashamed of his Baptist heritage. In Saddleback's membership classes he clearly communicates the church's affiliation with the Southern Baptist Convention.[24] Historically, Baptists have expressed their theology in "confessions of faith." The most widely accepted document is the nineteenth century *New Hampshire Confession of Faith*. Southern Baptists have revised this historic text many times over the years. Their *Baptist Faith and Message* is now the authoritative statement of Southern Baptist doctrine. Many observers believe that it has become so binding on Southern Baptist churches and institutions so as to function more like a creed, ensuring theological unity throughout the convention. Every Southern Baptist pastor knows the *Baptist Faith and Message.*

In writing the Saddleback doctrinal statement, Warren is rewriting the theology of his denomination. What Warren chooses to include, and what he chooses to exclude, reveal the weaknesses in his theology. Although we do not have the space to contrast the documents section by section, a single comparison ought to reveal the direction Warren is taking his church. The *Baptist Faith & Message's* statement on God says:

> There is one and only one living and true God. He is an intelligent, spiritual, and personal Being, the Creator, Redeemer, Preserver, and Ruler of the universe. God is infinite in holiness and all other perfections. God is all powerful and all knowing; and His perfect knowledge extends to all things, past, present, and future, including the future decisions of His free creatures. To Him we owe the highest love, reverence, and obedience. The eternal triune God reveals Himself to us as Father, Son, and Holy Spirit, with distinct personal attributes, but without division of nature, essence, or being.[25]

Compare that with Saddleback's statement:

> Many people have differing ideas about the nature of God. Most of those ideas have one thing in common—they are the product of human intellect! When it comes to our Creator, it matters very little

who we think God is. The Bible is the only trustwor-
thy source for understanding Him. Scripture teaches
that God created everything we can see—and even
everything we can't see—out of nothing. Although
it might be difficult for the human mind to comprehend, the Bible teaches that He is one yet has
existed since the beginning of time as three distinct
and equal persons: the Father, the Son, and the Holy
Spirit.[26]

Notice the difference between the two statements.
The Southern Baptist statement makes a series of positive
statements about God: "There is…He is…God is…" The
Saddleback statement begins with a statement of theological pluralism: "Many people have differing ideas about the
nature of God." It moves to a statement of the incapacity
of the human mind to discern truth: "Most of those ideas
have one thing in common—they are the product of human
intellect!" Then he says that theology is irrelevant anyway!
"When it comes to our Creator, it matters very little who
we think God is." Does it really not matter who we think
God is? Even the positive statements, such as describing
God as Trinity, are prefaced with the disclaimer that even
these things "might be difficult for the human mind to
comprehend…."

The tone of the two doctrinal statements could not be
more dissimilar. The *Baptist Faith and* Message speaks with
authority about what we can know about God. Saddleback's
What We Believe communicates that there are lots of different
theological opinions, and it really doesn't matter what we
think because we cannot comprehend it anyway. Presumably that is why Warren chose as his one sentence doctrine
of God: "God is bigger and better and closer than we can
imagine." That accurately sums up Saddleback agnosticism.

The Bible reveals some things about God, Warren says, but even those are difficult to understand. Really the only things we need to affirm about God are that he created everything, that he is three persons: Father, Son, and Holy Spirit, and that he "existed since the beginning of time."

According to traditional Christian theology God is eternal and immortal, but there is no mention of these qualities in Saddleback's statement. Warren has no statements about the infinity, eternity, or immortality of God. There is no mention of God's holiness, power, or sovereignty. Warren omits any reference to God as "Redeemer, Preserver, and Ruler of the universe." The *Baptist Faith and Message* refers to the traditional understandings of God as omnipotent and omniscient, but Warren makes no mention of them. Why all these omissions?

If Warren truly is unashamed of his Baptist heritage and affiliation, why didn't he just adopt the Southern Baptist confession of faith as his church's doctrinal statement? This is what the Southern Baptist Convention asks of its member congregations. Warren either does not agree with the *Baptist Faith and Message,* or he thinks it is unhelpful in his church's task to reach the lost. This would be consistent with the megachurch movement's theological amnesia. Megachurch expressions of Christian theology tend to be superficial. The role that doctrine plays in the life of the church is marginal at best.[27]

In short, the Saddleback statement is economy-size theology. He calls worship at Saddleback "deeply doctrinal,"[28] but the truth is that it is "doctrine optional." Warren says it is idolatrous to worship a politically correct and spiritually comfortable image of God, yet that is exactly what Warren has done.[29] The Saddleback God is a culturally comfortable, fuzzy deity that can be whatever you want him to be. It is like the images of the Virgin Mary that people discern in the formless patterns of knotholes, water stains, and half-eaten cheese sandwiches. If you know what you are looking for, and you look hard enough, you can see it there; but to the objective observer it is just an old cheese sandwich.

Purpose-Driven theology is like finding a pattern in the clouds. If you are an evangelical Christian, you can make out the image of the Christian God in Warren's writings—just barely—If you squint. But if you don't have knowledge of the biblical God, you can make it into whatever you want. *Purpose-Driven* theology has big gaps where doctrine ought to be. By filling in the gaps you can make it say whatever you want it to say.

Fill in the Blank Theology

One of the practices encouraged by Rick Warren is the distribution of sermon outlines to the congregation. Warren says that he never preaches without handing out a printed outline of his message. Upon his recommendation thousands of pastors now accompany their messages with printed outlines.[30] I have visited churches where I have been given a "fill in the blank" sermon outline. The outline has blank spaces in it, apparently so that there will be some suspense about what the preacher is going to say. For example: "God so _____ the world that he gave his only begotten Son." Sometimes the first letter of the missing world is supplied to make sure the congregation gets it right. "God so L_____the world...."

Whenever I am handed such an outline I feel like my intelligence is being insulted. In junior high school we begged the teachers to give us "multiple-choice" tests instead of the standard "question and answer" or the dreaded "essay question" exams. My favorite was a combination of "multiple choice" and "fill-in-the-blank." We called them "idiot tests," because any idiot could pass them. Whenever I am handed one of these outlines in a church I get flashbacks of Mrs. Roach's seventh-grade English class.

Rick Warren's theology is like these outlines. Not only is it simple, but also there are blanks where Christian doctrines ought to be. There are holes in Saddleback theology big enough to drive a bus of Mormon missionaries through. As a pastor, I teach more theology to twelve year-olds in my five-week baptismal classes. Surely the adult members of Saddleback Church can handle a complete statement of Christian doctrine! But we have to remember is that it really doesn't matter to Rick Warren or Saddleback Church. Saddleback is not about theology; it is about relationships.

Who is the Purpose-Driven Jesus?

The Christian's most important relationship is with Jesus Christ. Warren says that true life begins when you commit yourself to Jesus.[31] If there were any area of theology that you would expect to be accurate and complete it would be the understanding of the Savior. But what we find in Warren's books is an undefined Jesus. Knowing Warren's Baptist family background and his theological training at a respected Baptist seminary, I expected to find in *The Purpose-Driven Life* a description of the Christian life grounded in the person and work of Jesus Christ. Baptists are sometimes criticized for being too Christocentric—too focused on Jesus at the expense of the other persons of the Trinity. That complaint cannot be leveled against Rick Warren. Christ can barely be found in the pages of *The Purpose-Driven Life*.

It is clear that Rick Warren feels much more comfortable speaking of God in a generic sense, than talking about Jesus in a specific sense. Open up *The Purpose-Driven Life* to any page, and you can find fifteen or twenty references to

God. But you will likely find no mention of Jesus. Try it for yourself. The few statements he makes about Jesus are true, but they are scattered throughout the book as illustrations for more important points he is trying to make.

In Saddleback's single-sentence *What We Believe* statement we find only this single statement about Christ: "Jesus is God showing himself to us." In the more complete statement of faith, Saddleback confesses:

> Jesus Christ is God's Son and an equal of the Father. He has existed from the beginning of time, yet lived on earth during the first century A.D. Throughout His earthly life, he was completely God and completely human at the same time. After living a perfect, sinless life, Jesus offered Himself as the perfect sacrifice for every human being who has ever lived by dying on a Roman cross. After three days in the grave, he defeated sin and death by rising from the grave. He then ascended to Heaven and will return to earth one day to reign as King.[32]

This is not too bad, until you see what he chose to omit from Saddleback's doctrine of Christ. There is no mention of the Virgin Birth or that Jesus was conceived by the Holy Spirit. Even the early and very brief Christian declaration known as *The Apostle's Creed* says that Jesus "was conceived of the Holy Spirit, born of the Virgin Mary." But you will not find these truths affirmed by Saddleback Church.

Likewise there is no mention of the substitutionary atonement. Saddleback affirms that "Jesus offered Himself as the perfect sacrifice" but that is as far as it goes. That is not far enough. The Reformation was fought over the nature and extent of that perfect sacrifice. The Southern Baptist denominational statement correctly insists on stating that "in His substitutionary death on the cross He made provision for the redemption of men from sin." Warren makes no mention of the sufficiency or the nature of the sacrifice. But he does take the space in this condensed confession to affirm the universality of the sacrifice "for every human being who has ever lived," thereby refuting the Calvinist doctrine of limited atonement. From the beginnings of Baptist history in the early seventeenth century, Baptists have included both General Baptists and Particular Baptists, those who affirmed a universal atonement and those who held to a limited atonement. Yet the normally inclusive Warren goes out of his way to choose sides in this ongoing theological debate. Why would Warren be silent on important doctrines like the Virgin Birth yet insist on taking a stand on the Calvinist-Arminian dispute?

It is important to note that these two doctrines, the Virgin Birth and the substitutionary atonement, are two of the seven "fundamentals" of the Christian faith that historically defined evangelicalism as it diverged from theological liberalism in the late nineteenth and early twentieth century. If any one of the seven fundamentals were denied, it was deemed that the historic Christian faith had been compromised. Warren omits two in his doctrinal statement about Christ. He also denies the total depravity of man, the complete inability of man to save himself. If a church does not consider three of the seven evangelical essentials to be theologically necessary, is it still an evangelical congregation?

It is justifiable to say that Warren represents an evangelical neo-liberalism that is repeating the theological mistakes of the past. As one pastor and professor writes: "Liberalism is alive and well in many evangelical churches…This practical liberalism is undermining historic evangelical doctrine.

Confessing Evangelicals must deal with Neoliberal Evangelicals because the very heart of the gospel is at stake."[33]

What Must I Do To Be Saved?

The crucial weakness of Rick Warren's theology is his understanding of how we are saved through Jesus Christ. In his books Warren never explains the nature and person of Jesus. Reading *The Purpose-Driven Life*, you have no way to know who Jesus is or how to distinguish him from any other religious figure, such as Buddha or Muhammad. The *Purpose-Driven* Jesus is an undefined Christ. Readers of *The Purpose-Driven Life* are asked to commit their lives to Jesus without first being introduced to him. That is like signing a marriage license before meeting your future spouse.

In Warren's defense, he does explain a little about Jesus in his church's doctrinal statement. Warren calls Jesus "completely God and completely human at the same time." This is an affirmation of the traditional understanding of both the full humanity and full divinity of Jesus Christ. Unfortunately there is no corresponding statement anywhere in *The Purpose-Driven Life*. That is a serious weakness when your goal is to introduce seekers to the Savior and instruct them in how to follow him! It further emphasizes the fact that for Rick Warren, basic theology is not important, not even when it comes to accepting Jesus as Lord.

When it comes to Christ's work on the cross, the situation is even more worrisome. Scattered through *The Purpose-Driven Life* are well-known evangelical catchphrases like "Jesus died for you!"[34] and "He paid for our sins on the cross."[35] But those clichés are the full extent of this his presentation of the cross. He is writing for seekers who have no accurate knowledge of Jesus. But he never explains who Jesus is or how his death accomplished our salvation. As we have already seen, in the Saddleback creed Warren omits the concept of substitutionary atonement. Perhaps that significant omission could be overlooked if there were some other explanation of how the death of Jesus was sufficient for our salvation. That is never addressed in any format.

The *Purpose-Driven* Christ is a shadowy figure, undefined and unexplained. But that does not stop Warren from leading readers to commit their lives to Jesus and then assure them that they are eternally saved. *The Purpose-Driven Life* employs a form of psychological manipulation to get people to make a personal commitment to Jesus Christ without explaining who Jesus is, how he saves us, or what we must do (beyond praying a little prayer) in order to be saved.

Warren introduces *The Purpose-Driven Life* by explaining that this is not just a book the reader is holding in his hands. It is much more than a mere book; it is also a guide to a spiritual journey.[36] Before the reader has even read the first chapter, he is asked to sign a covenant with the author to devote the next forty days to studying this book. This is the hook. Once the reader has made this initial commitment, he is much more likely to make a subsequent commitment.

After the covenant is signed by both parties (Warren conveniently has already signed the document in advance with a facsimile signature), the first section of the book begins. It is entitled "What on Earth am I Here For?" The title page has a woodcut of a bridge crossing a river to a grassy bank upon which stands a tree. Two Scripture quotations from the Old Testament describe it as the tree of life. This tree becomes the theme of the book in later chapters. But the reader is not there yet. This section is the bridge (a well-known symbol of decision and transition) over which he is passing to that promised land of the purpose-driven life. The reader is on a journey. It begins with a week of explaining the importance of making God the focus of your life.

At the end of Day Seven, Warren invites the reader to accept Christ as Savior. He sounds like a revival preacher urging his hearers to walk the sawdust trail. He tells his readers that it is time to settle accounts with God, to decide to live for God instead of oneself. He invites the reader to make a decision now. "All you need to do is receive and believe."[37] "Receive and believe" is Warren's formula for salvation.

First the reader has to *believe*. He has to believe that God loves him. He has to believe that God made him for his purpose. He has to believe that he is not an accident. He has to believe that he was created to live forever. He has to believe that God chose him, Jesus died for him, and that God desires to forgive him.[38] That is it. There is no mention of believing anything about who Jesus is. No mention of believing in Jesus' resurrection, ascension, or return. There is no mention of grace or faith, no mention of what we are saved from or saved for.

Then the reader is asked to *receive*. Receive Jesus as Lord and Savior. Receive forgiveness of sin. Receive the Holy Spirit. Warren invites the reader to silently whisper this little prayer: *Jesus, I believe in you and I receive you.* Then Warren assures the reader that if he sincerely prayed those few words, he is now irrevocably a part of God's heavenly family.[39] With a simple prayer, the deal is closed, the bridge is crossed, and the reader is on the road to purposeful living. John MacArthur describes Warren's approach exactly: "Listening to a seeker-sensitive evangelical preacher today, we're likely to think it's easy to be a Christian. Just say these little words, pray this little prayer, and poof! You're in the club. According to the Bible, it doesn't work that way."[40]

Notice what is missing from Rick Warren's plan of salvation. There is no confession of sin or repentance. Hebrews 6:1-2 speaks of the "elementary principles of Christ" that are

the basics of salvation. The first on the list is "the foundation of repentance from dead works." Only then can one go
on to faith and baptism. Even the ministry and baptism of
Jesus was preceded by the baptism of John the Baptist, which
was a "baptism of repentance for the forgiveness of sins."
John scolded those Pharisees and Sadducees, who came for
baptism without repentance, saying, "Brood of vipers! Who
warned you to flee from the wrath to come? Therefore bear
fruits worthy of repentance" (Matthew 3:7-8).

Warren does not lay this foundation of repentance in his
presentation of the gospel. There is no turning away from
dead works, no call to bear fruits worthy of repentance. Just
believe a few platitudes, receive an unexplained Jesus, and
you are assured of eternal life. What a deal! Give up nothing and get a guaranteed ticket to heaven! Missing are the
challenging demands of Jesus. Omitted are any mentions of
self-denial and suffering, judgment, or everlasting punishment. The *Purpose-Driven* gospel is nothing more than a
postmodern version of the old time liberalism, described by
Richard Niebuhr as "a God without wrath [bringing] men
without sin into a kingdom without judgment through the
ministrations of a Christ without a cross."[41]

This is a far cry from the biblical message of salvation.
On the Day of Pentecost, the birthday of the church, the
apostle Peter preached to a multitude that rivaled the size
of the crowds at Saddleback. When the people heard Peter
explain who Jesus was and what he did, it says, "Now when
they heard this, they were cut to the heart, and said to Peter
and the rest of the apostles, 'Men and brethren, what shall
we do?'" Then Peter said to them, "Repent, and let every
one of you be baptized in the name of Jesus Christ for the
remission of sins; and you shall receive the gift of the Holy
Spirit" (Acts 2:37-38).

They were "cut to the heart." The Holy Spirit was convicting them of their sin. This is the Spirit's work in conversion according to Jesus: "And when He has come, He will convict the world of sin, and of righteousness, and of judgment" (John 16:8). God was stirring the hearts of the crowds on Pentecost, granting them godly sorrow for their sin and leading them to repentance. The apostle Paul describes it: "For godly sorrow produces repentance leading to salvation" (2 Corinthians 7:10).

For Warren there is no godly sorrow. That would spoil the upbeat mood of the seeker service. There is no repentance. There is no need to be convicted of sin in Warren's plan of salvation. Peter says to another crowd in the next chapter of Acts, "Repent therefore and be converted, that your sins may be blotted out" (Acts 3:19). There is no conversion in Warren's spiritual world; there is just a commitment. No need to get on your knees and cry out for mercy like the Philippian jailer, who was so distressed he was on the verge of suicide. There is no beating of the breast and crying out with the tax collector, "God be merciful to me a sinner" (Luke 18:13). In Warren's world you just need to bow your head and whisper a little prayer.

This is cheap grace. Commitment without confession is not conversion. Being "born again" without repentance is not genuine regeneration. Warren leads his readers into a superficial commitment with a false sense of eternal security. In Saddleback country all that matters is sincerity. "If you sincerely meant that prayer, congratulations! Welcome to the family of God!"[42] This is just a variation on the postmodern principle that "it doesn't matter what you believe as long as you are sincere." The truth is that sincerity is not enough. There needs to be a basic understanding of the gospel—of whom you are committing yourself to and what that commitment involves. Warren does not provide that minimal understanding before he asks for the commitment, nor does he provide it afterwards.

The reader is never told of the need to confess sins and to turn away from dead works. He is not told of the essential element of repentance before you can receive forgiveness. Only if we confess our sins will God be faithful and just to forgive us our sins and to cleanse us from all unrighteousness (1 John 1:9). Warren does not want to deal with the messiness of confessing sins. It is too long and complicated and painful. It is spiritual surgery, and Saddleback is not equipped for that. The megachurch is not a surgical center, but a first-aid station. So he applies a Band-Aid and says, "All is well." Warrens deserves the rebuke of the prophet Jeremiah who said of such preachers: "For they have healed the hurt of the daughter of My people slightly, saying, Peace, peace; when there is no peace" (Jeremiah 8:11).

Warren's "believe-and-receivism" is like planting the tree of new life without first digging a hole. Like the seed of Jesus' parable, which stayed on the surface of the ground and never took root, it will die. True conversion is a transformation. The old has to be done away with before the new can come. In Warrenism there is no genuine commitment to Christ because the genuine Christ has not been preached and the way of salvation has not been explained. "How then shall they call on Him in whom they have not believed? And how shall they believe in Him of whom they have not heard?" (Romans 10:14).

Clamshell Theology

There are other unbiblical elements in Warren's view of salvation. One is his faulty understanding of the nature of man, which results in a faulty understanding of the salvation of man. Warren says, "You are a spirit that resides in a body."[43] He says again, "Like God, we are spiritual beings—our spirits are immortal and will outlast our earthly bodies."[44] This is clamshell theology. It sees the spirit indwelling the body like a clam in a shell. This is Greek philosophical dualism. It comes from Plato, not Paul. It was one of the errors of Gnosticism, the heresy that challenged the early church.

In the biblical worldview man is not a spirit in a body. Man is a physical, psychological, spiritual unity. Man is just as much body as he is spirit. We are just as much physical beings as we are spiritual beings. That is why it was important that Jesus was physically resurrected and didn't just survive his death as a spirit. The risen Jesus said to his disciples, "Behold My hands and My feet, that it is I Myself. Handle Me and see, for a spirit does not have flesh and bones as you see I have" (Luke 24:39). This is why the biblical promise of the afterlife is not to be a disembodied spirit in heaven, but to be bodily resurrected.

Theological dualism always leads to moral relativism. If we are not really a body, then what we do in the body is not of eternal importance. This led some first century Roman Christians to "continue in sin that grace may abound." The apostle Paul replies: "Certainly not! How shall we who died to sin live any longer in it? Or do you not know that as many of us as were baptized into Christ Jesus were baptized into His death? Therefore we were buried with Him through baptism into death, that just as Christ was raised from the dead by the glory of the Father, even so we also should walk in newness of life" (Romans 6:1-4).

It is not surprising that Warren rejects the biblical understanding of man. It explains why he is unconcerned with confession and repentance. For if you are just a spirit in a body, all you need is a salvation of the spirit; you do not need to be overly concerned with the sins of the body.

Cooperating With God

Warren teaches that we cooperate with God in our salvation. For him salvation is a joint venture between the will of man and the work of God. This is not to say that Warren does not speak about the grace of God. Saddleback's doctrinal statement says, "Our disobedient nature has eternally separated us from our Creator. No matter how hard we try, we can never earn our way back into God's presence. Our only hope is to trust Jesus as God's provision for our disobedience. Whenever you make that decision, you step into the eternal and abundant life Jesus promises for all believers."[45] This statement clearly falls within the parameters of traditional Christianity—that salvation is a gift of God received through faith in Christ.

The problem comes when he explains how that decision for Christ is made and how salvation is worked out in our lives. The focus then shifts from God's grace to man's efforts. Warren explains the primacy of human initiative in the process of salvation in *The Purpose-Driven Life*, "God waits for us to act first."[46] Warren says that we first have to learn to trust Jesus, and then we will be invited to heaven.[47] Warren says that we have to cooperate with the work of the Holy Spirit.[48] He says, "Spiritual growth is a collaborative effort between you and the Holy Spirit."[49] In teaching pastors how to present the gospel with the greatest success, Warren tells them to "cooperate with what God is doing...."[50] Warren's biographer goes so far as to say that Warren teaches that heaven is a reward for following the teachings of the Bible and living an honest life.[51] That is an overstatement of Warren's position.

Warren avoids the works of Pelagianism (named after a 5th century Celtic monk condemned as a heretic) by making it clear that we cannot earn heaven solely by our own efforts. But he falls prey to a semi-Pelagian position that says that salvation is a cooperative venture between God and man. Thereby he moves away from the Reformation truth that salvation is "by grace alone." One Lutheran pastor concludes: "Upon careful study of this book, it is clear that Rev. Warren is a gifted author and I am sure a well-intentioned man, he has some helpful insights and practical advice, he emphasizes the uniqueness of each and every one of us, and that God has gifted each of us differently. However, he is, simply and plainly put, another in a long list of Semi-Pelagians."[52]

The Bible clearly says: "For when we were still without strength, in due time Christ died for the ungodly. ... God demonstrates His own love toward us, in that while we were still sinners, Christ died for us....For if when we were enemies we were reconciled to God through the death of His Son, much more, having been reconciled, we shall be saved by His life" (Romans 5:6-10). In God's Word, salvation is not received by being willing enough, strong enough, and favorably inclined toward God enough to act first and then cooperate with His love. Salvation is God acting first; indeed, it is God acting alone. That is the meaning of the Protestant doctrine of "grace alone."

Salvation is a gift of unmerited love granted to those without strength to take a step, to sinners "dead in trespasses and sins" (Ephesians 2:1), and to enemies at enmity with God (Romans 8:7). In the Bible, salvation is the gift of life given to sinners who are dead and can do nothing for themselves. "And you He made alive, who were dead in trespasses and sins, in which you once walked according to the course of this world ... But God, who is rich in mercy, because of His great love with which He loved us, even when we were dead in trespasses, made us alive together with Christ, by grace you have been saved" (Ephesians 2:1-2,4-5).

Salvation is by grace alone through faith alone. Paul continues his description of salvation in Ephesians 2:8-9 "For by grace you have been saved through faith, and that not of yourselves; it is the gift of God, not of works, lest anyone should boast." The error of much popular evangelical theology, including Rick Warren's, is that it is overly influenced by humanism, which focuses on man's abilities. Even the evangelical understanding of saving faith has been tainted with the American self-help culture. Three quarters of Americans believe that the Bible teaches, "God helps those who help themselves." Sixty-eight percent of "born-again Christians" believe that statement is true.[53] This is what seekers are looking for in a religion. Consequently they see faith as man's contribution to the salvation equation. Man seeks God, and God responds. God extends his grace and man closes the deal by placing his faith in Jesus. Faith is understood as man doing his part in his own salvation. To use Warren's terms, faith is man cooperating with God.

In the classic Protestant understanding, faith is not man cooperating with God. Salvation is purely the gift of God, and faith is nothing more than accepting the gift. Faith adds nothing to the gift, nor does it prompt the gift. There is a world of difference between the two understandings of faith. One sees man contributing something, however small, to the process of salvation. The other is man admitting that he has nothing to contribute. Faith is man opening his hands in prayer asking for undeserved mercy, and finding himself the unworthy recipient of the greatest gift ever given.

Without A Trace

When the apostle Paul came to Ephesus during his third missionary journey he came upon some disciples there. "He said to them, 'Did you receive the Holy Spirit when you believed?' So they said to him, 'We have not so much as heard whether there is a Holy Spirit'" (Acts 2:2). Warren's disciples might say the same thing. As you study *The Purpose-Driven Life,* you slowly notice that the Holy Spirit is missing!

Perhaps it is more accurate to say that he is hiding. He lingers in obscure corners of *The Purpose-Driven Life.* You have to search for any mention of him. When you find him, he plays only a supporting role. He is not the initiating, convicting, convincing, and regenerating person that Scripture describes. In the Bible the Holy Spirit "comes upon" people, usually unexpectedly and powerfully, like at Pentecost and in the "Ephesian Pentecost" of the Ephesian disciples. But for Warren, the Holy Spirit is the eternal gentleman; he will not come unless you invite him, always waiting for permission from man to act.[54]

Warren sees the role of man as allowing the Holy Spirit to change our way of thinking.[55] In the process of sanctification, we are not "being transformed" into the image of Christ "by the Spirit of the Lord" (2 Corinthians 3:18). Instead we cooperate with the Holy Spirit's work. The Spirit will not do anything unless we let him. We first have to change our minds, and then the Holy Spirit can come in and transform us with his truth.[56] The Spirit does not change us unless we change ourselves first. Warren teaches that the Holy Spirit does not release his power into our lives unless we first unlock God's power by acts of obedience. "God waits for you to act first"[57] Man's obedience, man's action, man's permission come first. The Holy Spirit becomes the lapdog of the Christian, tame and submissive. He is no longer the mighty wind and winnowing fire of the Bible.

Does It Really Matter?

We have been looking carefully at the theology of Rick Warren and his Saddleback Church. But does it really matter? Isn't being a Christian really just about accepting Jesus as Savior and following him as Lord? Do we really have to understand Christian theology to be a Christian? The prevalent attitude today is that theology may be important for preacher and teachers, but not essential for the ordinary Christian, unless you really want to get into your religion deeply. Presumably that is why Saddleback has one set of beliefs for the ordinary member and a further link for those who feel the need to go deeper. After all we all don't have a head for theology; what is important is having a heart for Jesus.

This theological relativism is demonstrated in how easily Christians can move from one denomination to another. It has been shown that people choose churches because of location, programs, music, and personality...not theology. People switch churches with hardly a thought to the fact they that they are entering a different theology, which may or may not be true to the Word of God. But that doesn't seem to matter. "After all, we all believe the same thing, don't we?" As a woman recently said to me, "We all worship the same God."

This easy ecumenism is caused by theological ignorance, which is a result of the dearth of doctrinal teaching in the churches. There was a time when Methodists and Baptists could come to blows over theological issues in town debates. Sermons and rebuttals would be printed in their entirety in the local newspapers. Today most Methodists and Baptists do not know enough of their own theology to articulate how they differ from each other, except perhaps that one sprinkles and the other dunks. There is a feeling among ordinary Christians that the doctrinal differences between Christians are the result of petty theological squabbling in the past, and they are irrelevant today.

People think it is a sign of Christian maturity to overlook theological differences and emphasize what we have in common. After all, we have common enemies to defend ourselves against: evolutionists, abortionists, secular humanists, and a host of foreign religions and homegrown cults! There is a feeling that we need to join forces for common social causes in what has been termed the "culture wars." The argument is that the moral decline of our nation behooves us to put aside our differences and join together for the good of the kingdom. It is argued that we can no longer afford the luxury of allowing doctrinal issues to divide us. That would be like playing chamber music while the Titanic sinks.

Pragmatic ecumenism has produced an evangelical culture in which doctrinal differences are glossed over in favor of a lowest common denominator theology. Denominational brand names are obsolete and are discarded with the old flannelgraphs. Warren, when he was starting Saddleback Church, did a survey of the community to find people's reaction to the label "Southern Baptist." He found it to have an almost universally negative connotation. His solution? Drop the label. He notes that people joining Saddleback Church are surprised to learn they are becoming Baptists. Most megachurches do not even bother with any denominational affiliation. They are fully independent "community" churches. Denominational connections are seen as encumbrances to growth; they are more trouble than they are worth.

Even evangelicals in the mainline denominational churches feel like they have more in common with fellow evangelicals of other denominations than they do with the "progressive" churches in their own denomination. This connection is strengthened by the huge growth of nondenominational parachurch organizations, ministries, publishing houses, and conferences. There is not a day that goes by that I do not receive announcements and advertisements for evangelical conferences, conventions, seminars, and literature—all of which are of much better quality than the low-budget counterparts of my mainline denomination. Many churches no longer use the educational materials published by their church publishing houses. Today Presbyterian, Methodist, and Baptist churches may all be using the same lessons in their Sunday school classes. As I write this chapter my church is using a nondenominational Vacation Bible School program. Driving around the community I have seen banners advertising the same program in front of Assemblies of God, Baptist, Lutheran, Methodist, and Presbyterian churches. What does that say about doctrinal distinctives?

Everything in the American evangelical culture, from Christian radio to Christian music to Christian celebrities, tells us that theology no longer matters. All that matters is whether you have a personal relationship with God, whether you have accepted Jesus as Lord and Savior, and whether you are born again. These are all understood in experiential rather than theological terms. The truth is that there is no relationship with God without a correct understanding of God. You cannot accept Jesus as Savior without understanding who he is and how he saves you. You cannot follow Jesus as Lord without knowing what the Lord requires of you. You cannot be saved without understanding the way of salvation. This does not mean that every Christian needs to take a seminary course in systematic theology. It does mean that the theological essentials need to be accurately communicated and understood.

George Barna, who for twenty-five years has exhaustively researched the connection between church and culture, has found that there is now a large group of people who call themselves "born again" but who have no understanding of basic Christian theology or ethics. He gives them the paradoxical label, "non-evangelical born-agains." They are not Christian in any identifiable sense except that they once walked the aisle at a Billy Graham Crusade, went through the pamphlet of Campus Crusade's *Four Spiritual Laws*, or whispered a little prayer after reading the first fifty pages of *The Purpose-Driven Life*. Barna calculates that only six percent of all adults, and seventeen percent of "born-again Christians," are genuinely Christian in what they believe or how they live.[58]

The evangelical label and conversion experience no longer describe the true Christian. We have entered an era of evangelicalism where those who would describe themselves as evangelicals may no longer be evangelical. The "evangel" (gospel) is missing from evangelism, and only an "ism" is left. At the forefront of this redefinition of evangelicals is the megachurch movement. The marshal of the megachurch parade is Rick Warren; its bible is *The Purpose-Driven Life*.

Theology does matter! It is the sidelining of theology that has gotten us into this evangelical quagmire. David F. Wells of Gordon Conwell Theological Seminary discerned this problem more than ten years ago with his book *No Place For Truth: Whatever Happened to Evangelical Theology?*[59] Today Christians live in an age when evangelicals are more socially visible and politically influential than ever before. But we have lost our soul, because we have lost our theology. Evangelicals are no longer distinguishable by a biblical theology and moral lifestyle. We are distinguishable only by where we go on Sunday morning and what type of music we listen to. Both of those are looking more like the world of secular entertainment. In truth the only difference between the evangelical and the pagan is the words *we sing*.

Evangelicals have become the mainline liberal Protestantism of the twenty-first century. We have become indistinguishable from culture. We are, as George Barna entitles his book on this topic, *The Frog in the Kettle*. The kettle has reached the boiling point and we are dead. We are the ghosts of our former Christianity. Like the Bruce Willis character in *The Sixth Sense*, evangelicalism is dead and doesn't realize it yet.

Does theology matter? Yes! It is just as important as making that personal commitment to Christ as Lord and Savior. Indeed without accurate theology there can be no true commitment to Christ. Without sound theology there can be no spiritual growth in Christ. Rick Warren in *The Purpose-Driven Life* has ridden the wave of evangelical culture and has become immensely successful. But what he is producing is cultural Christians with a conversionless commitment to a contentless Christ.

CHAPTER THREE

THE MARKET-DRIVEN LIFE

Rick Warren wanted *The Purpose-Driven Life* to be "more than a book." He has succeeded; it is a registered trademark. This is the first Christian book I have seen that carries a registration symbol ® in the title. The reader is regularly directed to an appendix at the rear of the book to purchase "Resources For the Purpose-Driven® Life," such as *The Purpose-Driven® Life Journal, The Purpose-Driven® Life Scripture Keepers* and *The Purpose-Driven® Life Album*. In Christian bookstores, you will find *Purpose-Driven* book covers, videos, wall calendars, t-shirts, caps, and musical CD's. You can even sign up for *The Purpose-Driven® Life Mobile Devotionals* sent directly to your cell phone.

Rick Warren's ministry is a merchandizing phenomenon. This is no accident; it is an integral part of the *Purpose-Driven* business plan. Rich Karlgaard, the publisher of Forbes magazine, calls *The Purpose-Driven Church*, "the best book on entrepreneurship, business and investment that I've read in some time."[1] Another writer for Forbes says: "Welcome to the megabusiness of megachurches, where pastors often act as chief executives and use business tactics to grow their congregations."[2] Both the philosophy and the vocabulary of the marketplace have been imported into the church. "Hence, using commercial marketing terms such as 'market segment,' 'niche,' 'satisfied customer,' even 'ROI' (return on investment) raises no eyebrows. In fact, such phrases trip easily off these pastoral tongues."[3] Warren's biographer says that Warren intentionally uses corporate terms like 'fill on demand,' 'downsizing,' merchandizing,' 'team players,' and 'niche marketing'"[4]

Christianity has become big business in America, and the megachurches are leading the way. Megachurches, defined as churches with at least 2,000 members, used to be few in number. In the last thirty-five years the number of megachurches has tripled and their "market share" has increased even more dramatically. Today, "half of all churchgoing Americans are attending only 12 percent of the nation's four hundred thousand churches."[5] We apparently like our churches "supersized," as well as our fries. Megachurches are the Wal-Marts of the religious market. The department store chain enters a community and lures away the customers of the local downtown merchants. Likewise the megachurches plant churches in the outskirts of town and grow by transfer of attenders from the dwindling downtown churches. The average American church, which has a congregation of less than 100 in worship, is going out of business at the rate of fifty a week, while the Christian supercenters are thriving.[6]

Why would people leave their local church on the corner, where their family has attended for generations, to attend a huge anonymous "worship center" that is a half-hour drive away? The answer lies in understanding the transformation of American culture in recent decades. Americans have come to see themselves primarily as consumers of goods and services. This attitudinal change has dramatically influenced the religious landscape. The roots of the small church no longer hold. Loyalty is easily transferred to a new church when it provides products and services more suited to the felt needs of the Christian. The American Christian has gone from being a disciple to being a customer, from being a follower of the Lord Jesus to being a consumer of a spiritual commodity.

The Culture of Consumerism

The megachurches didn't invent this consumer mentality; they are simply capitalizing on it. They did not cause this cultural shift, but neither are they challenging it in the name of a biblical worldview. They have made a conscious decision to play by the rules of consumerism, and they are gaining members in the process. What are the new rules of this spiritual capitalism? There are two of them.

Choice

First is choice, and lots of it. Immigrants to the United States are overwhelmed when they see the product choices we have in this country. Like fish in water, we who have lived here all our lives do not even notice it until we are taken out of it. Fifteen years ago I spent a three-month sabbatical leave on Israel's West Bank. My wife and I would take our three children on a mile hike to the nearest grocery store to replenish the kitchen cupboards of our small apartment. The whole store had two aisles about fifteen feet in length. The tiny market, run by a Palestinian family, had all we needed, but very few choices. If we recognized an American brand of breakfast cereal, we rejoiced. Compare that to the typical American supermarket where we have a difficult time deciding which cereal to buy because there are so many options. We are overwhelmed by choices.

Americans have come to see this plethora of choices as normal, and even as a right. If we want an ice cream cone on a hot day, we are no longer satisfied with Baskin Robbins 31 flavors. We have "designer ice cream" individually prepared for us to our exact specifications at Marble Slab Creamery. From cell phone ring tones to personalized credit cards, we define our lives by our choices. We create an image we wish to present to the world by the decisions we make concerning what we wear, what we eat, and what we drive. Our personal identity is wrapped up in our choices. Therefore it is not surprising that where we worship has increasingly become a matter of personal preference.

From the very beginning, America was pro-choice, religiously speaking. The early Puritans came to these shores in the seventeenth century to be free of the established Church of England. The American colonies thrived on religious tolerance. Baptists in particular were the champions of religious liberty. When other colonies compromised the freedom of religious dissenters by setting up their own established churches, the early Baptists founded Rhode Island to be a place of complete religious freedom. In time the Baptist vision dominated the land and was enshrined into federal law. Religion has thrived in the United States precisely because of the spirit of competition in the marketplace of religious ideas.

The present situation of evangelical consumerism is the result of this American proclivity for religious choice. Despite the rhetoric of the political left, no Christian today would want to deny freedom of religious expression to anyone. The issue is not whether or not we should have the right to choose. The question is the spiritual validity of our choices as judged by the biblical worldview. Are we choosing God's will or our own?

There is also the question of the willingness of churches to appeal to the basest instincts of man in order to draw a crowd. The megachurch movement in general, and Rick Warren's *Purpose-Driven* version in particular, have chosen to wholeheartedly adopt the marketplace mindset. "It is a mindset that cherishes the opportunity to choose, a mindset that expects to be served as the consumer....As a result [American Christians] view themselves as 'customers' in search of a religious product that can meet their felt needs and fulfill their desires."[7]

The typical church attender seems happy with this arrangement. They have voted with their feet, left the traditional church and embraced consumer Christianity. Americans have found in the megachurch a religion that will give them exactly what they want. If their "wants" change, the church will rapidly adjust to keep the customer coming back. This is only good business strategy. Warren has discovered that good business sense is also good church sense. What makes businesses succeed or fail applies also to churches. The key is good customer service.[8]

The Customer is Always Right

This is the second rule of megachurch success: the customer is always right. Our choices are treated as valid, no matter what they are. Private preferences are sovereign. "'Customer first' is more than just good business policy—it is a slogan that characterizes what American capitalism has come to expect. Sadly, many American Christians carry this attitude from the marketplace into the church."[9] No longer do Christians think that their choice of a church might be wrong. There are no wrong choices as long as it feels right. If it is meeting their expectations at the moment, that is all that matters. Customer preference reigns in the spiritual marketplace. Seekers seek places where their needs, wants, and desires will be fulfilled the best. No one in the mega-church dares question the legitimacy of seekers' preferences. If they did, their clients would find another church more to their liking.

This pattern of catering to the consumer confirms us in our egotism by giving us the impression that the spiritual life is really all about what we want. When this is affirmed in the megachurch with the assertion that we can serve both our desires and God, then the deception is complete. Such evangelicals have gone from bad to worse, "deceiving and being deceived" (2 Timothy 3:13). Church becomes all about us—selfishness sanctified in the name of Jesus. As Gebhards observes, "Today, however, the church is a place of self-indulgence and self-satisfaction. Self-interest has become pandemic, even in worship, making it difficult for some churchgoers to imagine that Christianity is not intended to revolve around them."[10]

Shuffling the Saints

"There is none righteous, no, not one," the apostle Paul quotes the psalmist as saying (Roman 3:10). Nowhere is this truer than in American religion. We cannot point a finger at the megachurch and think that we have "clean hands and a pure heart." We all have sinned. All churches market themselves, though they might cringe at the use of the term. The difference is whether we embrace the marketing enterprise as the driving force of ministry, or whether we treat it gingerly as a dangerous tool that has the power to corrupt the very nature of the church.

There has always been competition between churches in America precisely because we have no state religion. The consequence of religious freedom is that people can worship wherever and however they want; and those desires are seldom spiritually selfless. The best of men are still men at best. Men are sinners who do not seek God. "There is none righteous, no, not one; There is none who understands; There is none who seeks after God. They have all turned aside; They have together become unprofitable; There is none who does good, no, not one" (Romans 3:10-12).

Carnal men seek carnal churches. Unregenerate men will be attracted to churches that affirm their unregenerate desires. The churches that are most plainspoken in their proclamation of the scandal of the gospel will seldom be the ones bursting at the seams on Sunday mornings. Every pastor who has struggled with the tension between biblical preaching and budget balancing knows that to be the case. The intolerable truths of the gospel are toned down to accommodate the practical business of growing the church.

For Americans, bigger is always better, and growth is always good. This is a presupposition that is never challenged in church boardrooms, no matter how spiritual we consider ourselves to be. There is an assumption by clergy and laity alike that the best thing that could happen to their church is to bring more people into the worship services and more money into the offering plates. *How* it happens is not so important. *That* it happens is all-important. James Twitchell expresses the pastor's concern for survival: "From Monday to Friday you could pretend that you had your eye on Heaven, but over the weekend you had better be packing them in. Or you'd be sent packing."[11]

The reality is that the percentage of Americans who attend church regularly has not changed in thirty-five years. Although the expressed purpose of evangelicals is to evangelize the unchurched, the reality is that the percentage of the churched in society has remained constant. Some go, and some come; some are born and some die; some are baptized and some drift away. Converts come in the front door and out the back door in equal numbers. Even Rick Warren admits that he removes hundreds of members from his church rolls every year.[12] Though megachurches say they are reaching out to the unchurched, they have not made a dent in the demographics of Christianity. It is just a shuffling of the saints from one congregation to another.

New religious denominations arise and old ones decline. The new become the old, and newer ones arise. Megachurches are the latest chapter in this drama; they are the newest denomination on the scene. Although they may advertise themselves as nondenominational, they are in fact new denominations. Only the label has changed. Instead of being called Methodists or Presbyterians, they are "Willow Creek" and "Purpose-Driven." Like the older denominations before them, they plant churches that are networked together. These churches buy their educational materials and receive their Christian identity through the clearinghouse of the megachurch.

The only difference between the emerging megachurch denominations and the old mainline Protestant denominations is that the new ones have no clear theological identity or religious history. This is intentional; megachurches are self-consciously nondoctrinal and nonhistorical. This is both their attractiveness and their weakness. In an age when theology has become irrelevant, a church without theology is attractive. In a culture suffering from historical amnesia, religious heritage is extraneous. Rootless people seek a rootless church.

Marketing the Gospel

What megachurches lack in depth, they make up in breadth. One large church in western Pennsylvania is locally referred to as the "mile-wide church." This is not only because of its sprawling campus, but the impression that it is "a mile wide and an inch deep." No one could tell you want it stands for, but it is growing. I attended a pastor's conference at a large church affiliated with the Willow Creek Association. Willow Creek's founder and senior pastor Bill Hybels was the featured speaker. During lunch break, I sat with one of the ruling elders of the church. I asked him about his church's theology and polity. This middle-aged man, who had been a leader of the church for ten years, could not give me an answer! But his church was growing, and he was excited!

Megachurches grow by successful marketing. They view the world through the lens of capitalistic-style competition. Warren says that churches are in competition with the entertainment industry. To win people's attention the church has to give them something better than they can get elsewhere.[13] The philosophy of the megachurch is to compete with the world on its own terms and using the same strategies that businesses have found to work successfully. In the past the church has been reluctant to "sell" its product. That reticence has been jettisoned by the megachurch. The church now views evangelism as a marketing challenge. It markets its product like businesses market theirs.

Selection

The marketing of the gospel takes several forms. First is selection. The traditional meetings for worship and study of the Bible are not sufficient to grow a church. Churches now must broaden their product line beyond merely spiritual activities. Any church serious about outreach will build a "Christian Life Center" or a "Family Life Center." These provide space for any number of ministries from basketball, aerobics, yoga, childcare, bowling, counseling, and even fast food. Willow Creek Church has a food court that looks exactly like its counterpart in a shopping mall. The traditional fellowship around a coffee pot with a box of donuts has been replaced with Starbucks and biscotti.

The more serious a church is about marketing, the more products and services will be added to the church menu. The growing church has something for every age group and interest. There are evangelical recovery and support groups for every possible psychological malady and life crisis. There are special interest groups that focus on every conceivable avocation. There is literally something for everyone; if you don't see what you want, just put a note in the suggestion box. The church's aim is to please. Warren says that Saddleback is all about meeting needs. A church will only grow as long as it is meeting needs. He says that if a church follows this philosophy, then people will push down the door to get in, like a post-Thanksgiving sale at Macy's. The church would have to lock its doors to keep people away.[14]

Advertising

Advertising is the second element of church marketing. Historically, this is nothing new; megachurches are just taking it to a new level. When the advertising industry began to blossom in the early twentieth century, the innovators came from devout Protestant backgrounds. In a chapter entitled "One Market Under God," a professor of advertising lists the "early apostles of advertising." They were men like Artemis Ward, son of an Episcopal minister; John Wanamaker, a staunch Presbyterian who considered entering the ministry; Claude Hopkins, who came from a line of preachers; James Webb Young, a Bible salesman; and Helen Lansdowne, daughter of a Presbyterian minister and student at Princeton Theological Seminary. One of the most interesting is Bruce Barton, son of a Baptist preacher, who wrote a book in 1925 entitled *The Man Nobody Knows*, which describes Jesus as an advertising genius, selling redemption, busy about his Father's business.[15] Marketing the gospel is nothing new. As soon as the consumer culture began in the twentieth century, the Christians hopped on the bandwagon, drumming up business for the Lord.

The difference in modern megachurch marketing is that now the tail wags the dog. The goal of bringing people into the church building has become more important than the message the church proclaims. The audience, instead of the message, has become sovereign. In order to avoid rejection, the megachurch has made its message one that no reasonable person would refuse. Advertising is designed to stop people in their tracks and think about what is being promoted. Only a message that appeals to the needs of the consumer can do that.

The megachurch, in promoting ministries that meet every need, has become a bazaar. It takes little imagination to picture Jesus standing in the gift shop or food court of the megachurch brandishing a whip of cords. The gospel, if still present at all, is relegated to a sideshow. While the preaching of the gospel languishes, the church is filled with people busy with the fun and exciting attractions that the church has to offer. The megachurch has become John Bunyan's Vanity Fair. The megachurch is a religious mega-mall, a controlled environment of spiritual consumption with boutiques catering to every taste. It feels more like a theme park than a place of worship, more like a multiplex theatre than a sacred space.

We have become used to this "malling of religion." It feels natural to us. We have come to expect a good show. The "old, old story" is no longer sufficient for our tastes. We are a generation looking for signs and wonders, and the megachurch delivers. This has transformed our expectations of the church. Churches lure people with advertisements of excitement and entertainment. This succeeds only in producing an appetite for more dramatic performances from the church staff. Like Hollywood film producers striving for more fantastic special effects, churches search for more dramatic ways to draw a crowd. The presentation becomes most important. The truthfulness and the quality of the message are peripheral.

Choosing a Brand Name

As in all advertising, a good brand name is essential. The megachurch moniker is carefully chosen with the marketplace in mind. Warren describes the process he went through to choose a name for his new congregation. He surveyed the community and found that his denominational label "Baptist" had negative connotations, so he jettisoned the term. All churches with megachurch aspirations eliminate such references to theological or denominational heritage. They are seen as cultural baggage that gets in the way of growth. Sometimes churches will even avoid the use of words like "church" or "Christian," so as not to scare away potential attenders.

The word "community" has become popular in church names because it is so prevalent in the wider culture. The term has favorable connotations, yet has become so overused as to have no identifiable content. Newscasters will speak about "the gay community," and, paradoxically, "the homeless community." "Community" no longer means anything, yet it is has positive overtones. Therefore it is the perfect name for the church that wishes to offend no one. Other popular names include "fellowship" and "worship center," or perhaps just "Christian center." Often a geographical location attached to the word "church" is sufficient. Willow Creek Church, Garden Grove Community Church, and Saddleback Valley Community Church (often simply referred to as Saddleback Church) have all chosen that safe option. In these names a generic spiritual component is communicated without any content to put people off.

Physical Facility

Another important element of megachurch marketing is the physical facility. From the very beginning the megachurch eschewed the traditional church building. Robert Schuller chose a drive-in theatre for his venue. Most beginning megachurches choose hotel ballrooms or school auditoriums as their meeting place. Warren prides himself on the fact of that for the first fifteen years Saddleback Church had no building, while growing to an attendance of 10,000. During that period of time they met in 79 different facilities. He jokes that Saddleback was the church people could attend—if they could find it![16] You would think that this "musical chairs" approach would be detrimental to the growth of a congregation. But it was just the opposite. Once again, rootless society finds its narcissistic reflection in the rootless church.

When a megachurch finally builds a facility, it is as untraditional as the congregation. Megachurches look like theme parks. They are sprawling complexes surrounded with acres of color-coded parking with helpful attendants guiding you to your parking space. You almost expect to see Mickey Mouse hats on the smiling young men and women.

Recently a church with megachurch hopes near my home decided to move out of their traditional brick steepled building and into an abandoned food warehouse in a strip mall. In discussions with the town officials, the pastor assured them that the church did not intend to change the appearance of the building. When asked if the church would be offended if an "exotic dancing" club moved into the mall, the pastor assured the town fathers that they would have no objection. This reveals the mentality that is seeping out of the megachurches and into the local churches. Namely, that there should be nothing physically distinctive about the church. To reach people it needs to "break down barriers to growth," and anything that sets apart the church as different is a barrier to growth.

Architecture

The architecture of the megachurch is an expression of its inner life. Church buildings used to be topped by steeples pointing to the heavens. Cathedrals aspired upward toward God. Architects designed buttresses to support the walls allowing churches to grow taller while at the same time giving them a vaulted spacious interior. Frescos of the last judgment, the return of Christ, and eternal reward finished the effect that heaven was the goal of the worshipers. The message communicated by the architecture of the megachurch could not be more different.

The megachurch of today looks like a junior college campus or a shopping mall. The direction of the architecture is horizontal rather than vertical. The message is clear: they are reaching out, not reaching up. The inside of the megachurch is constructed like a theater, often complete with movie screens. There is nothing in the main "worship center" that would make you think you were entering a holy space. It is no longer a "sanctuary" but a replica of a secular performance center. The presence of a band warming up the audience completes the impression.

There are no pews. The elbow contact of the traditional church pew communicated fellowship and a connection to those beside you. The cushioned theatre seats and armrests in megachurches communicate individualized comfort. There is no pulpit. Often there is a bare stage with a barstool that suggests that a visit from a standup comedian is forthcoming. The expectation is not entirely inaccurate. When there is a podium at the front it is often made of transparent Plexiglas. Any furniture that might convey the religious authority of the speaker is removed. Barriers between speaker and audience are omitted in order to convey a sense of intimacy. The preacher invariably wears casual clothing and encourages the same in the congregation. Rick Warren wears his signature Hawaiian short-sleeve shirts intended to put the audience at ease. This is no clerical or professorial expert who will be addressing them; this is Uncle Rick stopping by for a chat.

Religious Symbolism

There are no religious symbols in megachurches. At Saddleback Church you will find no cross or other Christian symbolism. The main meeting area of Saddleback looks more like a sports arena than a church sanctuary. There is no cross or other traditional Christian images, no visual clues that might convey the Christian identity of the building. This is a common phenomenon among megachurches. Alan Wolfe describes his visit to Bill Hybel's megachurch, "Willow Creek. America's most famous megachurch, located outside Chicago, displays no cross on its building, but this does not mean it lacks one. 'We do have a cross,' as a tour guide explained. 'We bring it out for special occasions, like baptism.'"[17] Christian symbols are considered offensive to the average American, so they are removed. This is a concession to the popular opinion that any public display of Christian belief is a form of religious intolerance.

In the place of Christian symbols is vegetation, which itself is a powerful, though subtle, symbol of vitality and growth. The grounds of Warren's Saddleback church is meticulously landscaped with sycamores, Monterey pines, and a variety of colorful blooming flowers. Benches under palm trees allow the worshiper to rest on the way to the worship center. The purpose is to set the attenders at ease before they ever enter the main building. Another aspiring megachurch took this a little too far. The front of the auditorium was adorned not only with flowing green plants but also with Doric columns. I had the definite feeling I was entering a pagan temple from ancient Greece. I half expected to receive a visit from the Delphic oracle!

To complete this garden effect, two walls of the worship center of Saddleback Church are ceiling-to-floor glass, an effect Warren adopted from Robert Schuller's Crystal Cathedral. These transparent walls complete the feeling of horizontal space as well as connection to the Edenic gardens outside. Christian symbols are carefully extricated, as if by a Supreme Court order, from the interior of Saddleback Church, but quotations from *The Purpose-Driven Life* are everywhere. Although you will not find a pulpit Bible or pew Bibles, you will find phrases from the wisdom of Warren etched into the glass over the doorways, decorating the walls like verses from the Quran in a mosque.

The Bottom Line

In the megachurch the final word is the bottom line. Money speaks loudly in our culture, and this is true in the culture of the American megachurch. The market forces of American society have invaded the church and subjected it to the rule of mammon. Human beings are reduced to economic entities calling "giving units." Decisions are made on the basis of cost effectiveness. Staff members are judged by their productivity. Financial leaders trump the spiritual leaders. Everything is decided by the criterion of money. Money speaks loudly in churches of all sizes. In the megachurch this is embraced as a virtue, whereas in traditional churches it is seen as a necessary evil.

In my own congregation I saw the effect when our treasurer adopted new financial software that automatically labeled our church financial reports in terms of monthly and quarterly "profit" and "loss." Insidiously the profit mindset encroached upon the conversation about raising and saving money. Once the labels were changed, the discussions returned to a more godly perspective focused on ministry and stewardship.

Labels matter. Money speaks. Numbers rule. Success is measured in productivity. If the services rendered do not show up in increased numbers of customers served and dollars donated, then the message is adjusted to increase the bottom line. When Christianity is adjusted to people's expectations, then success is defined as numbers served and financial goals met. The integrity of the message becomes irrelevant. Then the church becomes something entirely different than it was called to be by Christ. The quantity of consumers and the growth pattern of the congregation replace the mission of the church. The gospel is silenced. Truth becomes expendable. Profit replaces the prophet.

The Pragmatic Roots of the Purpose-Driven Life

Behind the marketing compulsion of the megachurch is the philosophy called pragmatism. To understand Rick Warren's evangelistic methods, you have to understand his underlying philosophy of Christian pragmatism. The name comes from the Greek word "pragma," which means action. English words like "practice" and "practical" come from the same Greek root. Pragmatism is a philosophy that holds that the test of truth is the usefulness of the idea. To determine whether something is true or false you look at the consequences of the idea when it is implemented. If it works, it is good; if it doesn't work, it must be wrong.

Norman Geisler condenses the philosophy to this simple statement: "It works, therefore it is true."[18] When applied to actions it is summed up with the phrase: the end justifies the means.

Early Pragmatists

Pragmatism began in America in the late nineteenth century. Charles Sanders Pierce is considered to be the founder of pragmatism, when he proposed the concept in an article in 1878 entitled, "How to Make Our Ideas Plain." But the idea did not become popular until espoused by the religious philosopher and psychologist, William James, in an address delivered at the University of California in 1898. (Warren even quotes William James' famous statement on the ultimate act of pragmatism).[19] Pragmatism was adopted by John Dewey, the well-known philosopher of education, and became the foundation of the American public education system. A prominent Protestant advocate of Christian pragmatism was Reinhold Niebuhr.

Donald McGavran

Pragmatism entered into evangelical Christianity through the writings of Donald McGavran and the Church Growth Movement. As a son of missionaries in India, McGavran knew firsthand the frustration of missionaries who would dedicate decades of their lives to mission work with little fruit to show for all their sacrifice. He believed that missions could be done better. He dedicated his life to finding methods that worked in the mission field to grow churches. He found in the philosophy of pragmatism the intellectual framework to change the face of modern missions. He said, "We devise mission methods and policies in the light of what God has blessed—and what he has obviously not blessed. Industry calls this 'modifying operation in light of feedback.'...If it doesn't work to the glory of God and the extension of Christ's church, throw it away and get something which does. As to methods, we are fiercely pragmatic—doctrine is something else."[20]

You can hear clearly the influence of McGavran's pragmatism in *The Purpose-Driven Church*. Warren calls it "surfing spiritual waves." He says people ought to stop asking God to bless their ministries and start doing what God is already blessing, which he defines as what is bringing in the crowds. The objective of *The Purpose-Driven Church* is to teach the reader how to recognize what works and to implement those "principles and processes." Warren says he can teach pastors to discern what the Lord is doing and how to cooperate with him. This is surfing the waves of God's blessing.[21]

C. Peter Wagner

C. Peter Wagner is one of the foremost experts in the area of missions and church growth. He has served on many mission organizations and ministries. He taught with Donald McGavran at Fuller Seminary School of World Missions where he served as professor of Church Growth for twenty-eight years. He was founding president of the American Society for Church Growth. He has written more than sixty books on the topic. Wagner is outspoken in regard to the philosophical pragmatism of the Church Growth Movement. He calls it "consecrated pragmatism" and rightly warns that it must not compromise Christian ethics or doctrine. He writes, "The Bible does not allow us to sin that grace may abound or to use whatever means that God has prohibited in order to accomplish those ends He has recommended. But with this proviso we ought to see clearly that the end *does* justify the means. What else possibly could justify the means? If the method I am using accomplishes the goal I am aiming at, it is for that reason a good method. If, on the other, my method is not accomplishing the goal, how can I be justified in continuing to use it."[22]

Rick Warren is fully committed to Wagner's form of Christian pragmatism, but without the caution of Wagner. Warren justifies the sacrifice of living a life of Christian morality with an appeal to its rewards. In *The Purpose-Driven Life* he says that if there were no heaven or hell, then he would recommend that people just "live it up." They could forget about living according to God's will because there would be no consequences of their actions. We could indulge our basest desires without having to fear any eternal repercussions.[23]

The only reason that Warren sees for living a Christian life is because of the consequences after death! If God did not reward or punish us after death, then there would be no reason, in Warren's view, to live morally. The fact that it is commanded in the Ten Commandments does not matter. The fact that Jesus tells us to love God and our neighbor does not matter. For Warren, the motivation for ethical living has nothing to do with love or obedience. We obey solely because if we don't, we will have to face the consequences after death. In Warren's understanding of the spiritual life, the saints of the Old Testament, who had no clear promise of a heavenly reward, had no reason to live holy lives.

The Perils of Pragmatism

Pragmatism undercuts the foundation of Christian ethics and doctrine. It is a philosophy antithetical to the Christian worldview. The two cannot be amalgamated into a "consecrated pragmatism" or a "Christian pragmatism" without seriously compromising the Christian component. Nathan Busenitz calls pragmatism, and the seeker-sensitive movement based upon it, "a philosophical system that is inherently unbiblical."[24] John MacArthur is even stronger in his condemnation. "Pragmatism as a guiding philosophy of ministry is inherently flawed. Pragmatism as a test of truth is nothing short of satanic. Nevertheless, an overpowering surge of ardent pragmatism is sweeping through evangelicalism."[25]

Moral Relativism of Pragmatism

Why is pragmatism so dangerous to the Christian life and church? *First, pragmatism denies any absolute standards of right and wrong.* Pragmatism does not believe in moral absolutes. A behavior is not wrong by nature; it is only wrong if its results are perceived as bad. The action itself is morally neutral. In our American educational system designed by John Dewey it is called "values neutral education." Actions have no intrinsic moral nature. They are only practical or impractical; they are relatively good or bad depending on the outcome of the action. In *The Purpose-Driven Church*, any strategy that can bring seekers into the church is therefore good if it works. If it doesn't work, it is bad. In the Christian's life, a practice that brings a person closer to God is good if it works and bad if it does not. In *The Purpose-Driven Life* Warren can endorse many spiritual practices of questionable origin because where they come from does not matter. All that matters is whether they work.

In the biblical worldview, the moral nature of an action is not dependent on the results it produces; it depends solely on God's will. An action derives its moral character from the One who commands the action. It is not dependent on the outcome of the action. An action is good solely because it conforms to the will of God. In pragmatism, the end justifies the means; in the Christian worldview, God justifies the means.

Adultery, for example, is always wrong because it is a violation of the commandment of God, "Thou shalt not commit adultery." It is not considered to be right in some cases and wrong in other cases, depending on the results. Adultery is sin even when adultery, under extraordinary circumstances, may bring about a good result. This is why Joseph's Fletcher's *Situation Ethics* prompted such an outcry among evangelicals at the time it appeared in the 1960s. It was introducing humanistic pragmatism into Christianity, and evangelicals rightly rejected it. Today, pragmatism is heralded by evangelicals in the name of church growth. This shift reveals how far evangelicalism has drifted from its moral foundation.

Shortsightedness of Pragmatism

Second, pragmatism is shortsighted in its view of what constitutes a good end. It assumes that all growth is good. If a church is growing, then Christian pragmatism assumes it is the work of God. Observation belies this assumption. Islam is growing. Radical Islam that sponsors terrorism is the fastest growing part of Islam. Is that the work of God? The only mainline denomination that is growing is the Unitarian Universalist Association. Does that mean that God is blessing the abandonment of the doctrines of the trinity and eternal punishment? The Church Growth Movement studied all churches, regardless of their orthodoxy, and determined that certain principles worked regardless of theological stands.

From a biblical perspective it is clear that numerical growth by itself is not necessarily an indication of the endorsement of God. The prophet Elijah complained to God that, in spite of his faithful preaching, Baal worship was in the ascendancy in Israel and the true worship of God was declining. Elijah said he felt like he was the last remaining worshiper of God (1 Kings 19:14). Just because a religion is growing does not guarantee that God is behind the growth. Just because something does not produce growth does not mean it is wrong. There is more to what God is doing than what the numbers may say at the moment. God told Elijah that he still had a reserve of seven thousand in Israel who had not bowed their knee to Baal even though Elijah could not identify them to count them. Pragmatism has tunnel vision when it judges the validity of an action by the numbers it can count.

Pragmatism is also myopic when it comes to the time it takes to see results. Early pragmatism was much longer and broader in its determination of the amount of time it takes to produce a "good" end. Modern pragmatism, as adopted by the Church Growth Movement, follows our culture's desire for immediate satisfaction. It expects quick results or the strategy is abandoned as unfruitful.

In the Bible, growth is a slow process. It may not be seen in a lifetime. One sows and another reaps. Paul takes a long-term view of the work of evangelism and puts the results in God's hands. "I planted, Apollos watered, but God gave the increase. So then neither he who plants is anything, nor he who waters, but God who gives the increase" (1 Corinthians 3:6-7).

Jesus sees the work of proclaiming the gospel as deliberately inefficient and impractical in its means. In the parable of the Sower, Jesus likens the proclamation of the gospel to a man who scatters his seed in a very impragmatic manner (Matthew 13:1-9). He throws seed on the pathway. He throws it among stones and thorns. He also throws seed on good soil, which is the only soil that has a hope of producing a harvest. Christian pragmatism would never waste time, energy, and seed on unprofitable soil. It would concentrate efforts on the type of ground most likely to produce the best results. Even within the area of good soil, pragmatism would focus most attention on the soil that promised to produce hundredfold rather than the sixty-fold or thirty-fold.

God is not pragmatic; he does evangelism like the sower in the parable. If we are to do it God's way, we need to do it this way also. It is difficult for us to comprehend the reason for such divine inefficiency. Therefore Jesus follows the parable of the sower with a quote from the prophet Isaiah to help us understand.

> Hearing you will hear and shall not understand,
> And seeing you will see and not perceive;
> For the hearts of this people have grown dull.
> Their ears are hard of hearing,
> And their eyes they have closed,
> Lest they should see with their eyes
> and hear with their ears,
> Lest they should understand
> with their hearts and turn,
> So that I should heal them
> (Matthew 13:14-15; Isaiah 6:9-10).

Apparently it is just as important that people hear and reject the gospel, as it is that they accept it. There is a purpose for proclamation that goes beyond what can be measured in numbers of people who respond. Undoubtedly when people refuse to see and hear, it works together for a greater good that only God in his omniscience can see.

Pragmatism's Usurping the Role of Judge

The third peril of pragmatism is that it puts man rather than God in the position of judge. God has his reasons which man's reason cannot know. Yet pragmatism has no room for such faith. Pragmatism rests on the ability of man to see the goal and decide the best means to reach that goal. Christian pragmatism puts the sovereignty of man's judgment above the sovereignty of God. It assumes that man has the knowledge and foresight to see the possible good results of our actions and act accordingly. Experience teaches us that this is not true. We rarely can see anything but the most blatant and obvious results of our actions; even these we see through a glass darkly.

Christian pragmatism considers man as a freelance agent implementing the goals assigned to him by God. God is a divine CEO who sets the annual goals and gives his employees the freedom to devise strategies to reach those goals. At the end of the fiscal year all that matters is that the objectives are reached. On the other hand, in the biblical worldview the Lord sets the goals, which are only partially revealed to man. God then leads his servants to accomplish his divine purposes by guiding them in paths that may seem unclear at the time, but are later revealed as divine wisdom. We walk by faith as the Lord leads, not by sight as seems best to us. Pragmatism undermines such faith by teaching us to do what seems right in our own eyes. The fatal flaw of pragmatism is the sin of Eden, grasping the knowledge of good and evil rather than obeying God in childlike trust.

Pragmatism has a deadly effect when it comes to our personal relationship with Christ. Evangelical outreach has become dominated by the use of personal testimony. Biblical preaching is eclipsed by emotionally stirring stories by converts who share what Christ has done in their lives. The repetitive theme in such testimonies is how their lives have been changed for the better to produce family and financial well-being. Bill Hybel's program "How to Become a Contagious Christian" employs this model of personal evangelism.

It is true that Christ changes our lives for the better. We are also supposed to "always be ready to give a defense to everyone who asks you a reason for the hope that is in you" (1 Peter 3:15). But our salvation is not founded on personal testimony; it is founded on divine truth. The danger of the present emphasis on testimony as an evangelistic technique is that it emphasizes the pragmatism of the Christian faith. It proclaims, "Christianity worked for me; why don't you try it." We see sports celebrities give product testimonials on television; then we see them giving personal testimonies on stage at a Billy Graham crusade. The technique is the same: sell the product by affirming that it works. Try it; you'll like it.

What happens when Christianity fails to "work" in a person's life? Furthermore, what does it mean for Christianity to "work"? Does it mean, as Warren assures us, that it "will reduce your stress, simplify your decisions, [and] increase your satisfaction?"[26] The testimony of Scripture is that life is not easy, and salvation does not make it easier. In many ways commitment to Christ makes life more difficult, a fact that Jesus repeatedly pointed out to his followers. It means a cross and a sword. It means having no place to lay your head, giving up family, and receiving the scorn of men. Outside of America, becoming a Christian routinely means imprisonment, torture, suffering, and death. Christians inherit not only the blessings of Christ; we also inherit his cross and his enemies.

Before our conversion we drifted with the current of the world. Now we swim against it. Before Christ we lived as slaves to sin, the flesh, and the devil. We now must battle daily against these enemies of our soul. Before we knew Christ, the world would not persecute us because we were its own. But Jesus assures us that if we are his followers we will certainly suffer tribulation. In Revelation, the Beast only persecutes those who do not have his mark. Christians escape the wrath of God, but inherit the wrath of the devil, who knows his time is short and his end certain.

Christianity does not "work" from a temporal point of view. As the apostle Paul wrote, "If in this life only we have hope in Christ, we are of all men the most pitiable" (1 Corinthians 15:19). Christianity is not practical or pragmatic in an earthly sense. If we trust in Christ for his benefits to us in this life, then we will we disappointed and fall away when the going gets rough. We will not be able to persevere, which is one of the essential characteristics of saving faith. Evangelicalism has left thousands of dying souls in its wake by giving them a false hope of an easier life through Christ. These people now give a different type of testimony to their family and friends; they say that they are no longer Christians because "it did not work for me." Christianity is not pragmatic. Its truthfulness does not depend on its perceived effectiveness in a person's life. "Christianity is true, regardless of what works, and the propositions that support its truth are not based on personal testimonies."[27]

Pragmatism's Rejection of the Authority of Scripture

The fourth peril of pragmatism is that it undermines the authority of Scripture. When Scripture is sidelined, truth suffers. Canadian author and college professor, Laura Penny, sees the effects of pragmatism running rampant through all areas of life. "Never in the history of mankind have so many people uttered statements that they know to be untrue. Presidents, priests, politicians, lawyers, reporters, corporate executives, and countless others have taken to saying not what they actually believe, but what they want others to believe—not what is, but what works."[28] This is sadly true even in evangelical Christianity. People who know, for example, the truth of the wrath of God, will not speak of it for fear of sounding negative or judgmental and thereby "turning off" potential converts. "That is the essential message of the gospel, but in many contemporary gospel presentations there isn't even a mention of hell's existence. General William Booth, founder of the Salvation Army, warned that in the twentieth century a gospel would be preached that promised heaven without mentioning hell. Modern evangelistic methods do just that."[29]

In megachurches the truth of God's Word is abbreviated to adjust to what seekers want to hear. In *The Purpose-Driven Life*, Scripture is quoted copiously, but only to buttress the statements that will work in wooing seekers into the fold. It is never allowed to speak beyond the pragmatic parameters of the book. One man found out the hard way that there is no room for the Bible in the study of Warren's book. "A few months ago a friend phoned to ask if I had ever heard of Rick Warren. 'Yes' I replied. 'Why are you asking'? He said, 'I just got kicked out of a Bible Study for bringing my Bible to it....' The Bible study my friend attended was really a *Purpose-Driven Life* study group. The *Purpose-Driven Life* book they were studying referenced Bible passages that sounded off base. He was told that if he was going to attend the study, he would have to leave his Bible at home, because the issues he brought up were disruptive to the group."[30]

The Purpose-Driven Life does not use the Bible as an authority. It quotes it as a supporting witness when it is useful to do so. When the Bible is used in this manner, its authority is undermined just as certainly as if its cardinal truths were blatantly contradicted. This is why Jesus was so insistent that not one "jot or tittle" of the Old Testament was to be omitted (Matthew 5:18), and why the apostle John ends the Bible with a curse, warning the reader to add or omit nothing from his Revelation (Revelation 22:18-19). A gospel abbreviated to be more effective in reaching seekers is no gospel at all.

Pragmatism depends on man's experience, judgment, and reason to decide what is true and right. To be true to its nature, pragmatism must subordinate the role of Scripture to a supporting role. "The 'Christian pragmatist' will not hesitate to approach God's Word irreverently, taking a Scripture out of context to practically apply it to his or her life using allegory, 'spiritualizing' the text, etc., regardless of what God actually intended to communicate in the Scripture. This practice allows the person to make a Scripture mean anything he or she wants it to mean."[31]

I recently heard a message by Robert Schuller on his "Hour of Prayer" television broadcast.[32] The sermon was on 1 Timothy 4:14 "Do not neglect the gift that is in you...." He proceeded to give a message on how we receive and discover our gift. But not once did he read the rest of the verse, which tells exactly how Timothy received his gift! Schuller used a fragment of a verse as a springboard to deliver a message that had no biblical justification. How can a preacher employ such a blatantly illegitimate technique? He does it because it works! His audience was rapt with attention as he listed a myriad of ways to discover their "gifts" which had nothing to do with the gift of God to the young preacher Timothy "which was given to you by prophecy with the laying on of the hands of the eldership." If he had read the verse in context he would have also noticed that the previous verse says, "Till I come, give attention to reading, to exhortation, to doctrine" (1 Timothy 4:13).

The Gospel For Consumers

What is the gospel that consumers want, that fulfills Americans' felt needs and satisfies their inner desires? What is this gospel that seekers find so appealing that if preachers proclaim it, then so many people will flood through the church doors that pastors will have to turn them away?[33]

A Personalized Gospel

The consumer gospel is a personalized gospel. The gospel proclaimed from many evangelical pulpits has shifted from being *personal* to being *personalized.* The true gospel has always been about a *personal* relationship with a *personal* God involving *interpersonal* relationships with others in community. There has always been a place for *personal testimony* in the form of *personal* stories. The key difference between the historic evangelical gospel and this new megachurch personalization of Christianity and is that *personal* has come to mean *private.* The gospel has been privatized.

As I write this chapter, President George Bush is promoting his vision of privatized Social Security. Megachurch preachers are way ahead of him; they have adopted a privatized Christianity. The American "right to privacy" is celebrated in the megachurch. Christianity has become so privatized in the megachurch that the attender can remain anonymous. The seeker wants to keep a low profile, and that is what Rick Warren gives him. He tells pastors to permit visitors to be anonymous while in worship. People like to hide in a crowd.[34] To make people identify themselves is to "violate anonymity."[35] The church has become a place where anonymous individuals can feel comfortable in their anonymity while at the same time enjoying the illusion of community. "Church has become increasingly a private affair and a personal choice and less a place of real community at a time of growing fragmentation."[36]

The personalized gospel is a designer gospel, tailor-made with the individual consumer in mind. This is not the "one-size-fits-all" religion of yesteryear. Everyone does not have to believe the same thing or even worship in the same way. There are a variety of worship styles to choose from. Those who like pop contemporary music can attend one service.

Those who like a hard rock sound can attend a service in another room or another building on campus. Still others can opt for a more traditionally Protestant sound. These various worship experiences are often simultaneous and linked by video so that all can hear the same message on the screen when it comes time for the sermon. The megachurch aims to please.

This is true not only in regard to music but in theology as well. This is precisely why the doctrinal statements of such churches are so brief and vague. One church even asserts they have no creed except "Jesus is Lord." Under that vast umbrella, you are free to create a creed that fits your personal tastes. The result is designer doctrine that has no room for objective truth. In the megachurch, the individual has the opportunity to be part of a "Christian" congregation and yet believe whatever he wants, according to what he feels comfortable with. People are affirmed in what they already believe without being challenged by what is true.

A Packaged Gospel

The consumer gospel is a packaged gospel. The message of Christianity is packaged in a form that is attractive to the seeker. The megachurch, like any growing company in the marketplace, is selling an image. Watch the advertisements on television (or even now in the movie theaters) and you will notice that it is difficult to immediately identify what is being sold. The product is no longer "up front and center" as it was in the old days of advertising. The virtues of the product are not promoted; it is a self-image that is being communicated, in which the product plays a visible role. In megachurch marketing, the gospel is not being presented; it is being packaged. Essential parts of the gospel—conviction of sin, judgment, hell, and righteousness—are omitted.

Kinder and gentler aspects are brought to the forefront in a setting pleasing to the eye and the flesh.

The megachurch seeks to present an image of Christianity so attractive that the seeker will want to buy it. The problem is that what they purchase is the packaging without clearly seeing the contents. They buy into the megachurch mystique—the upbeat music, the comfortable building, the celebrity preacher, the inspirational testimonies, and the enthusiasm of the crowd. But the gospel somehow gets lost in the packaging, like an expensive pearl missing amidst mounds of wrapping paper on Christmas morning.

The professional packaging of Christianity in music, smiles, and special effects actually makes the gospel harder to hear. When the good news is swathed in smooth testimonies with happy endings and presented as the panacea for all your personal ills, can the scandal of the cross be heard? When does a market-adjusted gospel become so tailored to the expectations of the hearer that it ceases to be the apostolic truth?

The most serious danger of the megachurch movement is that this newly-minted megachurch gospel is being advertised as the same gospel that has always been preached by evangelicals. The reality is that it is not. It is a reincarnation of the old-time liberalism that infiltrated evangelical ranks a hundred years ago. MacArthur calls the megachurch gospel "the new modernism." He says that history is repeating itself. One hundred years ago evangelicals were caught off guard by a modernism proclaimed by those who identified themselves as evangelicals. They used the vocabulary of evangelicalism and gained a hearing from average Christians by their calls for Christian unity and tolerance. He sees the new modernism of megachurch Christianity following the same pattern today, and evangelicals are once again being taken by surprise.[37]

Repeatedly Rick Warren will insist that he is preaching the historic evangelical gospel, just presented differently for a new world. But the truth is that the world has so infiltrated his gospel that it has lost essential elements. The salt has lost its saltiness. It is no longer the evangelical gospel. It doesn't matter how stridently he insists he is evangelical; using the term does not make it so. Charles Spurgeon faced exactly the same thing in his day. Spurgeon wrote, "It is mere cant to cry, 'We are evangelical; we are all evangelical,' and yet decline to say what evangelical means." "You may believe anything, everything, or nothing, and yet be enrolled in the 'Evangelical' army—*so they say.* Will there arise no honest, out-spoken evangelicals among dissenters to expose and repudiate this latitudinarianism? Are all the watchmen asleep? Are all the churches indifferent?"[38] From the endorsements on the dustcovers of Rick Warren's books, it seems that the watchmen of American evangelical Christianity today are sound asleep.

CHAPTER FOUR

GIMME THAT SHOWTIME RELIGION

My family has been vacationing in a small New Hampshire town for decades. We had found a good evangelical church with contemporary music and a solid biblical preacher. Then, over the winter they called a new pastor. Our first Sunday he cajoled his wife to march down the aisle in a wedding veil to illustrate a joke. Then he showed a homemade silent video, starring himself, in the comedic style of Charlie Chaplin. The next Sunday he came to the front wearing a hard hat; there was a sign next to the pulpit that read "Construction Zone." He instructed three men to march down the aisle with paper bags over their heads as he illustrated a point. Later he had two volunteers duel with toy "light sabers" before the congregation. All in a day's work, or I should say, a day's preaching. I am not sure that the congregation understood what he was communicating, but the message I heard was clear: the gospel is boring and needs to be spiced up with entertaining antics to keep people's attention.

"In the course of a very few decades much of the church has embraced the way of mass culture in its drive to reduce everything to play and attractive entertainment."[1] The church is not alone in this march to amusement. Neil Postman wrote in his seminal book, *Amusing Ourselves to Death*, "Our politics, religion, news, athletics, education, and commerce have been transformed into congenial adjuncts of show business, largely without protest or even much popular notice. The result is that we are a people on the verge of amusing ourselves to death."[2] Middelmann calls this transformation of American religion "an extreme lightness of faith."[3] He says: "Our own generation has turned the Christian faith into something consisting of extreme lightness."[4]

I mourn the loss of authentic worship in the evangelical church. I need to worship; it is one of my strongest "felt needs." After a week in the wilderness of the world, I thirst for genuine worship in God's house with God's people. I do not need to be amused. I do not want to be entertained. I do not want to hear the same type of vacuous radio tunes I hear everywhere else. I expect the church to look, feel, and act differently. In many evangelical churches there is little difference. As Alan Wolfe says, "For the truth is that there is increasingly little difference between an essentially secular activity like the popular entertainment industry and the bring-'em-in-at-any-cost efforts of evangelical megachurches."[5]

I want to worship God; I do not want to applaud men. The congregational applause that now punctuates evangelical worship feels like a secular intrusion into sacred space. I feel like overturning some tables—or at least some padded chairs. I like to applaud at a concert or a theatre to show my appreciation for the performers. It feels sacrilegious to applaud worship leaders for worshiping God.

One week every year we attend a Southern Baptist congregation while visiting family in central Florida. (I now mark the visitor card "regular attender." I figure I have been attending there longer than most of the members.) I always leave the worship service feeling like I need to take a shower. The sticky sweetness of the performances clings to me. It is like rolling in a vat of cotton candy. I feel like I have been to a high school pep rally, and I need to find a place to worship as an adult. I get this feeling in a lot of evangelical churches.

The American concept of worship has changed. Rick Warren considers this a good thing. Warren describes the way he advertised the opening of Saddleback Church. When Saddleback was only a handful of believers meeting in his apartment, Warren sent out 15,000 letters announcing the first public worship service of the new congregation on Easter Sunday, 1980. The opening sentence of the letter stated that Saddleback was a new type of church for those who had given up on traditional worship services.[6] Warren has intentionally changed the understanding of worship.

In large sections of *The Purpose-Driven Life* and *The Purpose-Driven Church*, Warren spells out his new understanding of worship. Purpose #1 of *The Purpose-Driven Life* is all about worship. He states that there is not enough space in a single book to thoroughly explore the concept of worship, but he would explore the primary aspects.[7] Likewise Part Four of *The Purpose-Driven Church*, entitled "Bringing In a Crowd," is practical advice to pastors on how to design a worship service according to Warren's personal vision of worship.[8]

Expanding the Concept of Worship

First, Warren says that we need to expand our understanding of worship.[9] Warren begins by broadening the idea of worship in conventional directions. He lists the regular parts of traditional worship, such as Scripture, preaching, singing, and prayer. Then he says that even taking notes, greeting others, and signing a commitment card are actually forms of worship. [10]

Then Warren proceeds to broaden the definition of worship beyond traditional parameters. He says that worship is not a separate activity, but a lifestyle.[11] Every activity can be an act of worship when done for the pleasure of God. He quotes Martin Luther's comment that "A dairymaid can milk cows to the glory of God."[12] Worship is whatever makes God happy. Daily labor becomes an act of worship when it is dedicated to God.[13] Making love to your spouse can be an act of worship.[14] Even sleeping is an act of worship.[15] In that case, I have had some very devout worshipers in my congregations over the years!

Warren redefines the concept of worship so broadly that it can include anything! If everything can be worship, then worship is nothing in particular. The concept loses its meaning. This is the flaw of pantheism, which is a theological tendency in Warren's theology. If everything is sacred, then nothing is sacred. The sacred, by definition, must be set apart from the profane. If the sacred is no longer distinguished from the world, it has lost its sacredness. In the same way, worship is no longer sacred for Warren. Everything can be worship; therefore nothing is definitively worship. Worship has become indistinguishable from the world. Therefore it is not surprising that *Purpose-Driven* worship has become worldly.

The Bible divides the spiritual from the worldly. "Do not love the world or the things of the world. If anyone loves the world, the love of the Father is not in him. For all that is in the world—the lust of the flesh, the lust of the eyes, and the pride of life—is not of the Father but is of the world.

116

And the world is passing away, and the lust of it; but he who does the will of God abides forever" (1 John 2:15-17). The apostle Paul says: "Therefore I urge you, brothers, in view of God's mercy, to offer your bodies as living sacrifices, holy and pleasing to God—this is your spiritual act of worship. Do not be conformed any longer to the pattern of this world, but be transformed by the renewing of your mind. Then you will be able to test and prove what God's will is—his good, pleasing and perfect will" (Romans 12:1-2 NIV).

It is certainly true that all things can be done to the glory of God. Every act can be performed as an act of service to God. Warren is correct in wanting to bring spirituality out of the sanctuary and into the common areas of everyday life. We should do everything to the honor of God. It is admirable for milkmaids to milk cows for the glory of God! But that does not make it an act of worship. It simply makes it a way of glorifying God in daily life.

Worship is something different and should not be confused with daily work. It is something set apart. Jesus served God with his every activity, but he did not call them *worship*. He punctuated his normal activities with regular worship at the synagogue and the temple. In his conversation with the Samaritan woman about the nature of true worship in John 4, Jesus separated worship from any one particular place, either Gerizim or Jerusalem. He focused on how to "worship in spirit and truth," but he never suggested that the woman was worshiping God by giving Jesus a drink of water from the well! Jesus says elsewhere that such an act is worthy of reward (Matthew 10:42), but it is not worthy to be called worship.

Warren expands the concept of worship in an attempt to sanctify everyday life. He is employing the historic Protestant principle that menial labor has as much worth in the eyes of God as the "religious vocations" of monks and nuns. But in his attempt to sanctify everyday activities, he succeeds only in secularizing worship. Instead of making life in the world more godly, he makes worship of God more worldly. Worship becomes so infused with the profane that it loses its sense of the sacred.

Transforming the Experience of Worship

Warren's concept of worship has expanded to include the world of entertainment. Warren has *transformed worship into an entertainment experience.* He has embraced the Hollywood model of attracting crowds as a strategy for the church. Warren defends his strategy in *The Purpose-Driven Church.* He says that he has heard people say that the church is not the place to be entertained. For Warren, that is a shame. Most people think that church is boring. Warren wants to change that image. He sees nothing wrong with entertaining people in church. In his opinion the word "entertainment" has gotten a bad rap. Every preacher should strive to entertain. In fact he declares it to be a sin to bore people in worship![16] Back in the 1980s Michael Douglas articulated the secret avarice of many in the movie *Wall Street.* In that film, his character unabashedly proclaims his philosophy that "Greed is good." Warren has proclaimed to the Christian community: *Entertainment is good. Don't be ashamed of it. Embrace it!*

The typical worship service is seen as a place where you have to get dressed up and sit through an hour of ritual and listen to a boring sermon. The megachurch seeks to change that. It has made worship into a multimedia experience with live entertainment that keeps the audience's attention. Warren sees the worship service as a battleground for people's attention. He is not afraid to compete with the entertainment industry on its own turf. The church needs to entertain people better than the world does. He considers that the only way that the gospel can gain a hearing in today's world.[17] What Warren offers his congregation is a worship experience that has all the trappings of entertainment, but with a different message. But as McLuhan said, "The medium is the message." The vessel you use to communicate your message shapes the message communicated. Warren's form of Christianity is shaped by the means he employs.

Warren describes his preparations for the inaugural worship service of Saddleback Church as dress rehearsal during which they practiced the worship service.[18] The approach is like putting on a show. Warren's worship services are carefully planned to achieve a desired effect. He has even developed an acronym, IMPACT, to remind his staff of the effect they are trying to create.[19] Warren's worship services are carefully choreographed with exact timing, stirring music and powerful visual effects to meld the audience into a community sharing a common experience. A professional worship team guides the worshipers through a carefully orchestrated series of maneuvers designed to produce a spiritual encounter with God. On cue the people rise and sit, sway and pray, raise their hands and open their wallets. Nothing is left to chance, or to the spontaneous inspiration of God.

This is reminiscent of Charles Finney's revivalist approach to evangelism in the 19th century. He believed that there was a formula for success when it came to winning converts. If you presented the gospel in the proper manner, the crowds would walk the sawdust trail to the cross. Over the years he developed a method that "worked" and thousands came to the altar. Warren has developed a method that works; it produces results. The entertainment model has been proved successful in the secular world. In his typically pragmatic style, Warren has simply adapted it to work in the world of the church.

There was a movie some years back entitled *Sister Act*. It starred Whoopi Goldberg as a Reno lounge singer who witnesses a murder and decides to testify against her mobster boyfriend. Through the witness protection program she is given a new identity as a nun in a San Francisco convent. The parish is on the verge of shutting down; it needs a quick infusion of worshipers and cash if it is to survive. Whoopi's character, Sister Mary Clarence, decides to whoop up a hot new singing act for the worship service. Immediately it begins to draw a crowd. The film ends with a "standing room only" congregation and even the pope in attendance, swaying to the beat of the music. The message is clear. The church needs to pump up its worship program with music that gets the house rocking. That will bring in the crowd and the cash. This is exactly what Warren does.

In *The Purpose-Driven Church* Warren spends a lot of time on the church's music program. In fact he says that the only thing he regrets about the early days of Saddleback Church is that he did not spend more money on professional music.[20] Warren has implemented the "Whoopi worship" philosophy of church growth. He proudly reports that Saddleback is known as "the flock that likes to rock." He intentionally copies the type of music that draws the biggest crowds in the secular world. He deliberately chose his style of music to mimic the tunes that his members listen to on the radio.[21] He describes the Saddleback sound as "bright, happy, cheerful music with a strong beat."[22] Warren sounds like a teenager on Dick Clark's old television show *American Bandstand*. I almost expect him to add, "And you can dance to it."

According to a professor of preaching at Emory University, the typical megachurch praise song is "simplistic, repetitive, and, finally, boring…In the short run, it gets you on your feet clapping your hands, but in the long run it cultivates a monotonic, downsized faith, a faith too naïve and simple to handle complexity, too repetitive to deal with real change."[23] Yet in the short run the strategy works. Warren reports that within a year of adopting this popular style of music that his church "*exploded* with growth."[24]

But at what cost? People attend entertainment-driven churches because they are fun. You cannot find that as a distinguishing attribute of biblical worship. It is much more characteristic of the fertility cults that lured the ancient Israelites away from true worship. The joy of the Lord is fundamentally different than the entertaining fun of contemporary worship. *Purpose-Driven* worship uses the language of evangelical Christianity. The words of the songs are Christian. In fact Warren says that the lyrics are the only difference between Christian and non-Christian music.[25] But something substantive is missing. "The language of truth is still there, but the substance has been thrown away. Without any real truth, reality is turned into theater, and life into a show."[26]

Entertainment-based worship will bring people into the church. Entertainment-style preaching will keep people's attention; it can even bring people to make a commitment. It can change people's lives the way that a Tony Robbins motivational seminar can change lives. Hundreds of testimonies can be given as evidence of the success of the *Purpose-Driven* program. In true pragmatic fashion, Warren considers the "changed lives" as proof of the validity of his approach. He never asks the tough spiritual questions: How are they changed? By what are they changed? Every religion in the world can testify to changing lives. Programs like *Alcoholics Anonymous* are built on the testimonials of its adherents. But neither of these changes lives by the power of God.

The statistics of the Saddleback Church do not give witness to the power of God. Only a quarter of Saddleback members attend weekly.[27] That does not take into consideration the hundreds of members that Warren admits to purging from their church rolls annually due to inactivity. This percentage is half the average in the typical mainline Protestant church! Furthermore most of the inactive members of mainline churches have been on the church rolls for decades, as opposed to a few years for Saddleback. Warren boasts that 78 percent of his members come from unreligious backgrounds.[28] That is a dramatic claim. It needs to be verified by impartial research. It also needs to be demonstrated by sociological data that the presence of Saddleback Church has significantly altered the religious demographics of Orange County. My suspicion is that the Saddleback Valley is probably not very different than other Californian counties. They just have a better show in town.

Entertainment has the power to move people deeply. Music can transport people to places of beauty in their imagination. Films can move people to tears, and drama can stir people to action. Concerts can inspire people to act and to give. Celebrities can excite people as examples and role models. But the power of entertainment is no substitute for the power of the Holy Spirit. Showtime religion is no replacement for spiritual worship.

Jesus told the Samaritan woman that there is true and false worship of God. He bluntly told her that Samaritan worship was not genuine worship because they did not really know the God they were purporting to worship. "You worship what you do not know; we know what we worship, for salvation is of the Jews" (John 4:22). Jesus said that real worship was not connected with a place, but in spirit and truth. The Holy Spirit cannot be made to appear on demand by following the right methods. Neither the number of worshipers nor the intensity of worship indicates the truthfulness of the religion, as the failed worship of the prophets of Baal on Mount Carmel demonstrates (1 Kings 18). "True worshipers will worship the Father in spirit and truth; for the Father is seeking such to worship Him" (John 4:23).

Entertainment-focused worship has succeeded only in producing a new generation of "rice Christians." In the 19th century, Protestant missionaries soon learned that many of their converts came to worship only because it guaranteed them full stomachs. Seeker-sensitive churches have produced a crop of Christians who come to worship for the show. It feeds an emotional hunger for excitement. These Sunday morning productions are a caricature of worship. It is possible that sometime during the morning's performance the gospel might be heard and people saved. But more likely it is producing a generation of "rice Christians" who will cease to attend worship the moment their needs are no longer being met. Take away the show and the members will fall away like leaves in October. This is a mockery of worship.[29]

Secularizing the Space of Worship

By expanding the concept of worship into a Christian branch of the entertainment industry, Warren has *secularized the space of worship*. Go into a megachurch and there is no aesthetic sense of sacred space. Even the name of the place has been changed. The area where the saints worship is no longer a "sanctuary" but a "worship center." This loss of sanctuary is a significant transformation in American religion.

Sanctuary has many connotations. First of all, it signifies "holy space." That is the literal meaning of the word—a place that has been sanctified. Many religions have ceremonies that ritually set aside space for the exclusive use of holy activities. The word *sanctuary* has also come to mean a safe harbor from the dangers of life. In the Old Testament, the Law set aside "cities of refuge" throughout the Promised Land. They were a day's walk apart and served as "safe houses." The temple in Jerusalem was a similar sanctuary. When Adonijah failed to usurp the throne of Israel from his brother Solomon, he ran to the temple for refuge. If a man went into the temple courts and held onto the horns of the altar, he would be safe from harm (1 Kings 1:50-51).

Holy space is integral to religion. The Hebrew tabernacle, and later the temple, had a series of courts with increasing holiness, culminating in the Holy of Holies. Sacred objects and symbols marked the way into the presence of God. The megachurch has abolished such sacred architecture. The church is now an open space, both literally and symbolically. As you enter into the main meeting area of the megachurch, you get the feeling of large horizontal space focused on an empty stage. There is no indication that this area is dedicated to God. Instead, one gets the impression that it is dedicated to the entertainment and comfort of man. The padded seats, air-conditioning, lighting, sound system, video screens, music stands, and portable podium communicate a sense of a professional theatre. The closest thing to it in the ancient world was the amphitheatre.

Visit the ruins of any ancient Mediterranean city, and you will find the biggest structure in town was the amphitheatre. They could hold as many as twenty thousand people and were acoustically sophisticated even by today's standards. Utter a whisper at center stage, and you can be heard on the upper tier of the stadium. Compare that to the traditional Protestant church, where people complain that they can't hear even with electronic amplification! The ancient amphitheatre was the center of town life. Dramatic productions were presented there. Concerts were performed there. Government gatherings were held there. But no religious ceremonies were conducted there. Plays *about the gods* were performed in the amphitheatre, but worship *of the gods* was reserved for the temples and shrines.

In American evangelical Christianity, the church has become an amphitheatre. It is a secular space for crowds to be entertained rather than sacred ground upon which to worship. In fact the modern megachurch is more than an amphitheatre; it is an agora and hippodrome as well. Middelmann likens the megachurch to the Roman Coliseum, which was used to entertain the citizenry and distract them from the problems of the day. In the same manner, the megachurch more closely resembles a circus than a house of God.[30]

The Silencing of Silence

The sacred silence of prayer is replaced by the noise of the crowd. Warren purposefully eliminates silence from his seeker-sensitive worship service. He explains that silence is scary to the average American. He wants to create a welcoming atmosphere where people feel comfortable. Warren recommends that churches remove the silence and fill the space with noise—the louder the better. Saddleback has learned that the louder the background music is played, the louder people talk. He equates that loudness with joy and happiness. So now he pumps up the music as loud as he can. The last thing, you want in the worship service, he says, is silence.[31] A service is to be programmed with no "dead space" or "down time." One part of the service flows immediately into the other so there is no opportunity for silence to settle in.

In commending this practice, Warren is following the lead of American society. Silence is being systematically eliminated from public areas. It is as if a "No Silence" ban has been imposed by judicial decree. Yesterday I bought an ice cream cone at the outdoor window of an ice cream shop. I could not hear the vendor's questions because of the blare of music coming from the exterior sound system. There is music not only in the elevators, but also in malls, airline terminals, even in restrooms. It appears that even the privacy of the toilet is more than we can bear! Music used to be a special attraction; now it is the background noise of our lives. It is a way to protect our psyches from the uncomfortable sound of our own souls—or the voice of God.

Elijah went into the empty places of the wilderness to meet God at Mount Horeb. On the mountainside outside Elijah's cave there was a "sight and sound" multimedia display that surpassed anything Saddleback could produce. There was a hurricane, an earthquake, and fire. But the Lord was "not in the wind," "not in the earthquake," and "not in the fire." The special effects did not communicate the presence of the Lord. God was in the "still small voice." The Amplified Bible translates it "a sound of gentle stillness." The Lord was in the silence (1 Kings 19:12).

Removing silence from worship eliminates the still small voice of God. The Word of the Lord is drowned out by the cacophony of praise music. In the Old Testament Holy of Holies, God did not dwell in an image, but in the space between the cherubim. God dwells in empty spaces. If you fill the space with crowds of people and their friendly noises, then seekers might feel more comfortable, but God has no space to speak.

Profaning the Lord's Day

The loss of sacred space is accompanied by the loss of sacred time. Since New Testament times, Sunday has been "the Lord's Day." For the Christian community it paralleled, but did not duplicate, the role of the Jewish Sabbath. There was one holy day out of the seven. It was sacred time. With the secularization of sacred space has come the desacralization of time. The traditional eleven o'clock worship hour is inconvenient to the busy schedules of seekers and believers alike. So churches plan early Sunday services so the whole day would not be "wasted." Better yet is the Saturday evening service so Sunday can be set aside as a family day. The family has become sacred. Christian radio instructs us to *Focus on the Family*. Quality time with loved ones is our most valued commodity in American society. Time with the Lord is scheduled around work and family appointments. Evangelicals protest the removal of the Ten Commandments from public spaces, but the Sabbath commandment was long ago erased from evangelical schedules.

The megachurch is a 24/7 proposition. It is a full-service operation. The busyness of the megachurch campus is attractive to Americans who see bustling activity as a sign of success. It effuses an aura that something important is happening. There are so many people busy about the Lord's business! Surely the presence of the Lord is in this place! If he weren't, why would all these people be here? Rubbing shoulders with these bustling saints will certainly cause the spirituality of the place to rub off on us!

The sacredness of rest is foreign to the megachurch culture. The fourth commandment sets aside the seventh day as holy to the Lord. "The Lord blessed the Sabbath day and hallowed it" (Exodus 20:11). We are to "remember the

Sabbath day, to keep it holy" (Exodus 20:8). The Sabbath is kept holy by ceasing from profane activities, the chief of which is work. The Christian Lord's Day is not a legal replica of the Jewish Sabbath, but it has inherited the same sense of holiness. The Lord's Day was sanctified, not by creation or the exodus from Egypt like the Sabbath, but by the resurrection of Jesus. Since New Testament times the Lord's Day has been a holy day of fellowship and worship. As far as possible it also became a day of rest. The Sabbatarian practices of early Protestantism were nearly as strict as the Pharisees' Sabbath rules. This is not true of the *Purpose-Driven* form of evangelicalism. Rick Warren boasts of preaching twelve services in one day for the 25th anniversary celebration of his congregation. Saddleback is open for business seven days a week. The *Forty Days of Purpose* do not include a day of rest.

Casual Christianity

Warren's theological emphasis on the immanence of God has a practical counterpart in his style of worship. Rick Warren has transformed the worship of God into an informal get-together. Worship is like stopping by the house of a good friend rather than boldly approaching the throne of grace. The practice of "casual Fridays" in the workplace has been translated into "casual Sundays" at church. Everything about the *Purpose-Driven* church is casual.

This is the era of casual Christianity, and Rick Warren has embraced the trend wholeheartedly. He says that the word *formal* carries negative connotations. It means *phony* and *insincere*. On the other hand *informal* is equated with *authentic*. Warren wants his church to have this feeling of authenticity. So he has discarded reverential titles for himself and other staff members. He is not "Dr. Warren" but just plain "Rick." He says that Saddleback has no dress code. That is not exactly accurate. Its dress code is casual, and Warren models the code every Sunday with his preaching wardrobe. He says that clothing is a cultural issue, not a theological one.[32]

What clergy and congregation wear to church may not be a theological issue, but it translates into a theological attitude. When schools want to instill an attitude of respect in their students, they institute a dress code and insist on titles of respect for faculty and staff. They know that informality breeds contempt. We have found in our congregation that teen ministry requires that the youth pastor *not* be perceived as the kid's buddy, but an authority figure worthy of respect. Discipline deteriorates when boundaries are not clearly defined.

The casualness of worship translates into a casual understanding of God and a casual attitude toward God. Warren worships a casual God. In *The Purpose-Driven Life*, Warren rejects terms for God that might convey authority. He says the idea of an authoritative God is outdated. That would be making God into a slave driver, bully, tyrant, and dictator. The *Purpose-Driven* deity is not like that. Warren's God is a nice guy who would never try to enforce his will upon us. Instead he "woos us to himself." He is our brother and our friend.[33]

The Purpose-Driven Life's section on worship includes the chapter entitled, "Becoming Best Friends with God." It starts saying that God wants to be our best friend. For Warren, the ideal relationship with God is that of "intimate friendship" like what Adam and Eve had with God before the Fall. He asks us to imagine a relationship with God without rituals or ceremonies, no religion, too. (Do I hear echoes of John Lennon?) There is just simple love between God and man, unencumbered by fear or guilt.[34] *Purpose-*

Driven worship focuses on establishing, maintaining, and celebrating this type of Edenic relationship with God.

Warren's description of the goal of the Christian life actually seems to transcend friendship and approach a romantic relationship. At Saddleback Church, worship is defined as "expressing our love for God."[35] He says Saddleback's worship songs are actually love songs to God.[36] I can hear Rick Warren singing "Silly Love Songs" with Paul McCartney.[37]

You might think people have heard enough silly love songs, but apparently Rick Warren doesn't think so.

These relational metaphors are biblical themes worthy to be developed. Moses and Abraham were called friends of God. Jesus said to his disciples, "No longer do I call you servants, for a servant does not know what his master is doing; but I have called you friends...." (John 15:15). Solomon's romantic *Song of Songs* has long been interpreted as an allegory of the soul's love for God. But the idea of Christian intimacy with God tells only part of the story. This is the repeated weakness of *Purpose-Driven* spirituality. What Warren says is not 100 percent wrong, but it is only half true. The counterbalance to these ideas is not presented.

If you are going to talk about the immanence of God, it has to be accompanied by a discussion of the transcendence of God. The closeness of God must be balanced with the otherness of God. Warren defines God as "closer than we can imagine," but never mentions the other side of the divine equation. God is also further than we can imagine. He is our "who art Father *in heaven*." God is the transcendent Lord of the universe. Warren says, "God is bigger and better and closer than we can imagine," but the truth is that Warren's God is too small. He can only be seen up close.

Also, our friendship with God is not automatic and cannot be taken for granted. It was bought with a price while we were enemies of God (Romans 5:10). There are those today who would call themselves believers who are in fact "enemies of the cross of Christ" (Philippians 3:18). James scolds his readers saying, "Adulterers and adulteresses! Do you not know that friendship with the world is enmity with God? Whoever therefore wants to be a friend of the world makes himself an enemy of God" (James 4:4). The concept of falling in love with Jesus needs to be balanced with a holy fear of God. Hebrews says, "It is a fearful thing to fall into the hands of the living God" (Hebrews 10:31). The idea of God as friend needs to be balanced with the understanding of God as holy.

The Strange Absence of Prayer

The ironic thing about *Purpose-Driven* worship is that God is *spoken about* in intimate terms, but he is seldom *spoken to* during worship. There is a strange absence of prayer in evangelical worship. The oddest thing about contemporary evangelical worship, both in the megachurch and in small congregations, is the disappearance of public prayer. There is a lot of talk about having a personal relationship with God, but no one wants to get too personal with him in public. There are occasional prayerful interjections by a worship leader, usually in rapture at the end of a beautiful song or to bless an offering. But any extended time of prayerful communion with God has gone the way of the necktie. Evangelicals talk all around God, but not to him—at least not in public.

Warren does not advocate the complete abandonment of prayer in worship, but he warns pastors to keep their pastoral prayers short, because people cannot handle long prayers. He says that if pastors pray too long, people will fall asleep. Warren ridicules intercession as nothing more than praying "for sister Bertha's ingrown toenail." He says that pastoral prayers are just ways for lazy pastors to "catch up on their quiet time."[38]

What strange things to say about the greatest privilege of the Christian! We have the honor of bringing our petitions before the throne of God! What could be more exciting than that? What is more important for pastors than modeling prayer for their people? What is more important than teaching seekers how to pray? The disciples besought Jesus, "Lord, teach us to pray!" But Warren wants to avoid public prayer so as not to slow down the service and scare off potential disciples.

Purpose-Driven worship is an odd mixture of singing love songs to God and being tongue-tied if we have to speak to him. Something is seriously wrong with this attitude toward worship. It resembles a form of celebrity stalking. Evangelicals are obsessed with God. They sing about him, talk about him, and sing silly love songs to him. But once the music fades and they are face to face with our Loved One, they lose interest in speaking with him. There is something spiritually unhealthy about this situation. People who are truly seeking God do not get bored when given an opportunity to talk with God. If they do, they are not seeking to worship; they want to be entertained. They are not seeking God, but a God substitute.

My personal assessment of most contemporary evangelical worship is that it is an ingenious substitute for worship. It is like artificial sweetener. It looks like sugar, tastes like sugar, and actually tastes sweeter than sugar! One brand even boasts of being made from the same substance as sugar, but it has no nutritional value. That is my assessment of much of contemporary worship. It looks like worship and tastes like worship; in many ways it tastes sweeter than worship in traditional Protestant churches. But it is not worship; it is a worship substitute.

Evangelical worship seems designed to distract worshipers from having direct contact with God. Just when God is about to speak, the worship leaders make some more noise to get our minds back on the show. The space between the cherubim is filled with idols. Singing about a personal relationship with God becomes a way of avoiding such a relationship. The illusion of spirituality is strong in evangelicalism. We get together and sing about God and his purpose for our lives, but it does not fill the God-shaped void in our souls. Only worship will do that. Warren echoes the evangelical cliché that Christianity is not a religion but a relationship.[39] But evangelicalism has become simply a religion that celebrates relationships, while being careful to avoid having to get intimate with God.

Personalizing the Style of Worship

A distinctive element of *The Purpose-Driven Life* is the *personalization of worship*. The word *personal* is omnipresent in the evangelical vocabulary. But the word does not have the meaning it once did. Whereas it used to mean the opposite of *impersonal*, now it is a synonym for *individual*. Warren says that worship is the private expression of the individual's love to God.[40] Worship is something that the individual does in his own special way, the way that satisfies his personal "felt needs."

According to the *Purpose-Driven Life*, if worship does not satisfy you, the problem must be the style of worship. You just have to mix it up a bit, make some changes, and you will be right back on track. Warren relates how his friend Gary Thomas observed that many Christians were stuck in "a worship rut" that did not satisfy their needs. He says that people should not force themselves to use worship styles that do not seem to work for them. God made every individual with a personal worship style. You just have to discover what it is.[41]

The *Purpose-Driven* solution to stale worship is not to address possible problems in the person's spiritual life that may be hindering true worship. Warren's solution is to alter the style of worship. He recommends Thomas' book *Sacred Pathways*, which presents nine different worship styles based on psychological personality types. Warren says there is no right approach to worship, just whatever is right for you.[42] This is designer Christianity, worship tailored to your personal preferences.

Gary Thomas's approach is very similar to the yogic ways of religious devotion described by Huston Smith in *The World's Religions*. For the Hindu, there is no single way to approach God; there are many paths to the divine, depending on the temperament of the worshipper. Smith, an advocate of Eastern religious philosophy, describes the Indian understanding of salvation. "Some people are primarily reflective. Others are emotional. Still others are active and energetic. Finally, some like to experiment."[43] There is an intellectual way of devotion called Jnana Yoga for the intellectual; a devotional way, Bhakti Yoga, for the emotional; a meditative way, Raja Yoga, for the contemplative; an active way, Karma yoga, for the active; and a physical way, Hatha yoga for the athletic.

Compare this to Warren's description of the various ways to worship. In the *Purpose-Driven Life*, he says that ascetics approach God through actions. Caregivers do it through love. Enthusiasts celebrate God. Contemplatives adore God. Intellectuals approach God through their minds. [44] Different strokes for different folks. There is no single way to approach God. It is unlikely that Warren is aware that he is endorsing the Hindu view of spiritual pluralism. But the reality is that they share a common understanding of how one approaches God. For Warren, Thomas, and Smith, there are many ways to worship. The important thing is to find a way that works for you. This fits perfectly with the individualism of American religion.

In the Bible, especially in the Old Testament, God prescribes a specific way to approach the Holy One of Israel. Variation was met with punishment, even death. Korah and his cohorts found this out when they decided they could worship their own way (Numbers 16). Uzziah, king of Judah, learned this lesson the hard way. "He sought God in the days of Zechariah, who had understanding in the visions of God; and as long as he sought the Lord, God made him prosper" (2 Chronicles 26:5). But he got bored with his role as king and wanted to worship in the Holy Place like the priests. Azariah and the priests "withstood King Uzziah, and said to him, 'It is not for you, Uzziah, to burn incense to the Lord, but for the priests, the sons of Aaron, who are consecrated to burn incense. Get out of the sanctuary, for you have trespassed! You shall have no honor from the Lord God" (2 Chronicles 26:18). When Uzziah refused to leave, the Lord struck him with leprosy. A similar thing happened to Moses' sister, Miriam, when she decided that she ought to have equal standing with Moses in the prophetic ministry (Numbers 12). There was one way of approaching God in the Bible, and it was not a matter of personal preference.

In *Purpose-Driven* spirituality, variety is the spice of life. The philosophical pragmatism, which informs *The Purpose-Driven Life*, presupposes that anything that works for you is right for you. This is a personalized form of consumer spirituality that operates on the assumption that personal tastes reign supreme. You can approach God any way you want. All that matters is that it is satisfying to the worshipper. This is an expression of the human desire to be the focus of attention. This is the type of attention given to the customer when making a purchase. And it carries over into Warren's form of consumer spirituality. But it is inappropriate in our dealings with God. How we approach God is not a matter of personal preference; it is a matter of divine imperative.

The alternative to personalized worship is not to retreat to the rituals or language of former generations. Warren observes how traditional churches are stuck in the past. They ask people to sit in 17th century pews, sing 18th century hymns sung to the sound of a 19th century organ. He correctly observes that many churches are out-of-date.[45] Warren is a little mixed up when it comes to his centuries. Pews became common in the 16th century, and the pipe organ dates from the 15th century! But he is right in his assessment of the church's resistance to change.

Churches tend to get stuck in old ways of doing things. "We never did it that way before" is a refrain heard too often in church boardrooms. We keep pouring the new wine of the gospel into the old wineskins of out-of-date practices and are surprised when we come up empty. This does not mean we should exchange the tyranny of tradition for the tyranny of personal preferences! There is another option: Spirit-led, rather than personal-preference-driven worship! Contemporary music and worship forms can be legitimately used to reach people with the gospel. But they must be a God-inspired forms of worship, not people-pleasing forms of entertainment.

The Sidelining of Scripture

The only thing more disturbing than the removal of prayer from evangelical worship is the sidelining of Scripture. If you attend a contemporary worship service today, you will not find any Scripture readings in the program. Mainline Protestant worship still maintains a weekly regimen of Scripture lessons. There will be a Gospel Lesson, an Epistle Lesson and usually an Old Testament Lesson. Often there is a Psalter Reading, read responsively or in unison. The use of the lectionary in mainline churches assures that the congregation will be exposed to large portions of the Bible during the church year. Mainline preaching, if not always doctrinally sound, will usually reference the sacred texts.

That is not the case in the megachurches or the small evangelical churches that follow their lead. Evangelical Christianity pays lip service to the Bible, but you will not find the Bible on the lips of people in the service. There is a strange absence of Scripture in evangelical churches and megachurches. There is no Bible on the pulpit or Bibles in the pews; indeed, there are usually no pews or pulpits! In the traditional Protestant sanctuary, the pulpit was front and center with a huge Bible resting upon it. The symbolism was clear: the Word of God is central in this church! My father-in-law, a Baptist preacher, even had his pulpit bolted to the floor so that it could not be moved for special church programs! His message was clear: nothing replaces the proclamation of the Word of God in this church!

In the contemporary worship center, the praise band and worship team are at center stage. The podium (it no longer has the name or the appearance of a pulpit) is a light piece of furniture that is not sturdy enough to hold a pulpit Bible. It is designed to be easily moved out of the way; it only comes into view when it is time for the pastor to give his "talk."

In contemporary evangelical worship, the Bible is no longer publicly read as a separate item in the order of worship. If read by the preacher before his message, the

Scripture passages tend to be brief and almost always from the New Testament. Often Scripture passages are not read before the message, but are included as part of the sermon. This reveals the changing nature of evangelical preaching, which is seldom an expository exploration of a biblical passage. Scripture verses are used as supporting evidence for the points instead of the foundational authority for the sermon. The message is filled with stories and anecdotes, punctuated by video clips and dramatic presentations. The sermon at Saddleback Church is broken up into three segments so as not to be too burdensome for the congregation to bear all at once.

For all the evangelical rhetoric about the authority of the Bible, the Bible is not treated as authoritative in evangelical worship. It is used more like a sourcebook of illustrations that has some helpful tips to guide us through the journey of life. The Saddleback statement of doctrine refers to the Bible as the "perfect guidebook for living."[46] One gets the impression of a motorist driving purposefully through the English countryside with his trusty guidebook on the seat beside him, ready to be consulted for traveling directions, interesting facts, and historical information.

Let Me Entertain You

Scripture has been removed from its central place in evangelical Christianity, thanks in large part to the influence of the megachurch movement. It is the evangelical consensus that lengthy biblical readings slow the pace of the service, so they are eliminated. Expository sermons bore the daylights out of seekers, so they are replaced with stories and practical biblical principles.[47] Warren says that most people are looking for relief, not truth.[48] So that is what the he gives them, a message light on truth and strong on relief from the pressures of modern life. Prayer is removed from the worship service to save time for more important things. Contemporary rock/pop music with Christian lyrics flashed on karaoke screens fills both the worship time and the visual space of the worship center. Dramatic productions, multi-media presentations, and professional performances by singers round out the rest of the hour.

The worship style of the *Purpose-Driven Church* is wildly successful. The religion business is booming because the church has learned that quality entertainment draws a crowd and brings in the cash. The entertainment model of worship has changed the very nature of evangelical worship. It has taken the focus off God and onto the performers on the stage. In many traditional churches the organist and choir were invisible. I grew up in a church where the choir loft was *behind* the congregation and the organist hidden from view. In the megachurch the musicians are the stars of the show.

The band is already playing as the congregation gathers. When the worship begins, the pastor is nowhere to be seen. The "worship team" is the opening act whose job is to warm up the crowd. The atmosphere of the service is that of a Christian music concert. Emotions soar, hands are raised in praise, closed eyes indicate that private prayer is happening, while the guitars gently weep. There may be a dramatic presentation by actors. A personal testimony may be given. There will usually be a solo performance followed by thunderous applause.

After the music sets the mood, the guitars and microphones are put away, and the keynote speaker comes on stage. The screen projects him to the congregation as larger than life. His message is outlined conveniently on the large screens that dominate the auditorium. There are fill-in-the-blank inserts in the program to help you follow his points. His message is brief, practical, and above all, interesting. Illustrations dominate. Seminary preaching classes teach that illustrations are windows that shed light on a biblical text. If that is the case, then the megachurch message is a glass house. There is so much light that the Scripture can no longer be seen. But it works. People respond. The church grows. Entertainment rules.

CHAPTER FIVE

SPIRITUAL BUT NOT RELIGIOUS

I'm spiritual but not religious." This is one of the slogans of popular American spirituality. These are the types of people that Rick Warren targets. His *Saddleback Sam* is skeptical of "organized religion." He may say that he believes in Jesus, but he doesn't like the institutional church.[1] Rick Warren shares their view of traditional Christianity. From the very beginning, Saddleback Church was envisioned as a new type of church for those who had given up on the traditional church.[2] When speaking of mainline Protestant pastors he portrays them as stodgy Pharisees and Sadducees.[3] He considers denominational labels as "negative baggage."[4] When he uses the term *religion* it is in a derogatory manner. "Jesus said, 'I have come that you might have life' (John 10:10). He didn't say, 'I've come that you might have *religion*.' Christianity is a life, not a religion...."[5] In *The Purpose-Driven Life* he explains to seekers that Christianity is not a religion, but a lifestyle.[6]

This is the "spirit of the age." It is the worldview of the average unchurched American. It is popular to be "spiritual but not religious." In *The Transformation of American Religion,* Alan Wolfe reports that many Americans do not identify with any one religion. Instead they draw from many different spiritual traditions "from traditional religions to New Age consciousness and ecological wholeness." They prefer to turn to unaffiliated spiritual teachers like Scott Peck and Thomas More for spiritual advice. He reports that the category of "spiritual but not religious" is now the fastest growing segment of American religion, having more adherents than either Catholics or Baptists.[7]

To be *spiritual* means that you are interested in religious ideas and practices, but have not identified with one religion. In good post-modern fashion, the "spiritual" person is open-minded, loving, and tolerant of all spiritualities. He has his own beliefs, but doesn't try to *force* them upon others by suggesting that theirs may be wrong. He respects the ideas and practices of all religions and has no problem linking up with them when it suits his purposes. Rick Warren's *Purpose-Driven Life* is part of this American spiritual milieu.

Purpose-Driven Mormons

USA Today reported, "Warren's pastor-training programs welcome Catholics, Methodists, Mormons, Jews, and ordained women." In the interview, Warren said, "I'm not going to get into a debate over the nonessentials. I won't try to change other denominations. Why be divisive?"[8] Pastor Randy Childs, concerned about the acceptance of non-Christian groups as part of a Christian seminar, wrote to Marty Cutrone, Saddleback's National Campaign Director. Cutrone replied:

Rick understands and acknowledges that Mormons are non-Christian Cultists. But he IS NOT implying here that we are embracing their erroneous doctrine when we welcome these other religious leaders to our conference....He's saying, in my opinion, that we're going to be completely open and welcome graciously any non-Christian cult leadership team to attend any of our PDC events. These PDC events provide a wonderful forum for Christian churches of any denomination, as well as non-Christian cults to join us for a presentation of the biblical model for the church. We are not endorsing these cults by allowing them to participate. Rather, we are building bridges and fostering dialogue about these biblical principles...that may in fact not only expose them to the truth, but they may even be persuaded by the Holy Spirit to respond to the truth. Furthermore, the PDC conf. isn't the appropriate forum to debate doctrine with non-Christian cults...P.S. I happen to know that a "New Age Church" up in Oregon implemented the 40 Days of Purpose this last fall... and I absolutely applaud this. I hope and pray their people read and heard the truth, and come to a saving knowledge of Jesus. To have discovered this and banned them from participation, would have been a travesty and done nothing but create ill will, and not given the Holy Spirit an opportunity to impact hearts.[9]

The willingness of Saddleback Church to embrace non-Christian groups reveals one of the most disturbing aspects of Rick Warren's model of ministry. The distinction between truth and error is of secondary importance in the *Purpose-Driven Church*. "Building bridges and fostering dialogue" are more important than confronting "erroneous doctrine."

The fact that Warren considers the theological differences between Mormons, Jews, and Christians to be
"nonessentials" is troubling. The fact that he considers
"debating doctrine" to be "divisive" is upsetting. The fact
that Saddleback's national campaign director would "absolutely applaud" the instruction of a New Age church on
how to gain more converts could be considered aiding and
abetting the enemy.

If The Foundations Are Destroyed

How did this happen? How could one who considers
himself a Southern Baptist and an evangelical Christian
come to the point where he sees nothing wrong with teaching Mormons and New Agers church-growth techniques?
Psalm 11:3 says, "If the foundations are destroyed, What
can the righteous do?" The foundations of evangelical
Christianity are being eroded by the gradual assimilation
of non-Christian philosophies into the framework of the
faith. Now there remains only an external resemblance to
historic Christianity.

I used to own an old house in the New Hampshire
woods, built in the nineteenth century by a veteran of the
Civil War. Over the years, carpenter ants took up residence
in the sills and rafters. Repeated visits by the exterminator
did not remedy the problem. Finally I called in a carpenter.
As he began to dismantle the ell, the true situation was
uncovered. What looked like solid wood on the outside
was, in fact, a hollow shell held together by a veneer of
wood and paint. Under the surface the timbers were rotten
to the core. This has happened to evangelical Christianity.
It looks like historic Christianity on the outside, but when
you start to examine its inner parts, you discover rot. The
foundations of evangelical Christianity are being destroyed.

The megachurch is replacing them with substitute building materials that will not stand when the storms arrive.

"But these churches are growing! Growth means life, doesn't it? Isn't the success of the megachurches evidence that God is blessing them?" This is exactly what Warren claims. But rapid growth does not necessarily mean health. Cancer grows much faster than healthy tissue. Paul says that false teaching spreads like cancer in the church.[10] In a forest, toadstools grow faster than any vegetation. They appear overnight, full-grown and colorful. But they feed on the decay of rotten trees. In the same way the megachurch is growing out of a decaying evangelicalism.

Jesus told a parable of two houses—one built on rock and the other on sand. Undoubtedly, the beach house was much nicer; after all, it was waterfront property! It certainly was built more quickly than the rock house. The builder did not have to spend all that time excavating and setting the footings on the bedrock. The beach house was probably bigger and fancier. All the money saved on the foundation could be put into more square footage and amenities. But when the storms came, the sand house fell, and the little rock house stood. "But why do you call Me, 'Lord, Lord,' and not do the things which I say? Whoever comes to Me, and hears My sayings and does them, I will show you whom he is like: he is like a man building a house who dug deep and laid the foundation on the rock. And when the flood arose, the stream beat vehemently against that house, and could not shake it, for it was founded on the rock" (Luke 6:46-48).

The storms are coming. This nation has enjoyed the unprecedented luxury of religious freedom for centuries, but we may not always be so blessed. Persecution is striking most other parts of the worldwide body of Christ. Why do we think we are immune? The Bible says that all who follow Christ *will* suffer persecution (John 16:33; 2 Timothy 3:12). The twentieth century was proclaimed "The Christian Century" by the periodical of the same name. They foresaw a hundred years of growth for the American church, and they were right. The twenty-first century may be "the post-Christian century" in the United States. The popular spirituality of popular American culture has the potential for infiltrating and undermining the Christian church and leading it into an era of apostasy. Christianity could easily become a form of godliness without its spiritual power (2 Timothy 3:5). I believe this is already happening, and the megachurches are leading the way. "If the foundations are destroyed, What can the righteous do?"

Pop Goes the Gospel

What is this new spirituality? It is most commonly referred to as the *New Age Movement,* but that term is gradually being replaced with others. It is sometimes called the *New Spirituality.* Those using Christian terminology will call it the *New Gospel.* Most often it is simply referred to as *Spirituality,* an inclusive term used to designate a mystical worldview found in all the religions of the world. The fact is that there is no label that is accepted by all its adherents. It goes by a variety of names and includes many organizations. The only thing these various parts have in common is a spiritual worldview that can be found in popular culture at all levels. Just as there is *pop* music and *pop* psychology, this collection of spiritual ideas is *pop spirituality.* The vast majority of the adherents will not identify themselves by the term *New Age,* but it remains the only term commonly used to describe this diverse movement.

It is not an organized religion; there is no headquarters, creed, or single spiritual leader. It is a network of groups and movements. But there are certain common traits that most of them share. They tend to be *anti-organized religion*, which usually means *anti-Christianity*. They will draw upon the esoteric teachings of Western mystics and employ some of the contemplative practices of Eastern Orthodoxy and Roman Catholicism, but they reject the exclusivity of traditional Christian religion. They are particularly disdainful of "fundamentalism," under which they group both Islamic terrorists and the Christian "religious right."

They are *anti-doctrinal*. They see theological statements of absolute truth as an immature form of religion. Like the Gnostics of the early Christian centuries (which they include as their spiritual ancestors), they see creeds as rigid and legalistic, an indication of undeveloped and unsophisticated spirituality. It is fine for neophytes, but the mature person moves beyond literalism to metaphorical understandings of Scripture. In the place of objective truth is subjective experience. Their spirituality is fundamentally *experiential*. They are extremely eclectic and pragmatic when it comes to spiritual practices that produce spiritual experiences. Do whatever works.

In this light they are *radically ecumenical* when it comes to networking and cooperating with other groups that share their basic assumptions. They tend to be grassroots in organizational structure. They are global in perspective. When politically active they tend to be environmentalists and advocates of global peace brought about by international cooperation. The earth is often referred to as sacred, and all people are one. Although some groups advocate some form of world government, others endorse a more local and individual path to global harmony.

Many practice Eastern physical exercise such as yoga and Tai Chi. When it comes to science and technology, they gravitate toward natural holistic medicine and organic foods. Popular interpretations of quantum physics, which dissolves the boundaries between individual objects and persons, fit well into their worldview. Their primary emphasis is personal spiritual growth, which is often linked to psychological self-fulfillment. They are individualistic and syncretistic, combining various spiritual beliefs and practices into a personalized spirituality.

Douglas Groothius, in *Unmasking the New Age,* sees six common philosophical ideas.[11]

1. **All is One**, known as *monism.* "All is interrelated, interdependent and interpenetrating. Ultimately there is no difference between God, a person, a carrot or a rock."[12]
2. **All is God**. "This is pantheism. All things–plants, snails, books and so on–are said to partake of the one divine essence."[13]
3. **Humanity is God**. Man is essentially divine. We are by nature one with God. We just need to wake up to this eternal truth.
4. **A Change in Consciousness.** The fundamental problem of humankind is ignorance. We need to be enlightened. By spiritual discipline the conscious awareness of Oneness with the divine can be achieved.
5. **All religions are one.** All religions are various expressions of the same Truth taught by different spiritual masters throughout the millennia. Jesus, Buddha, Muhammad, as well as the Dalai Lama and modern gurus, all teach the same truth expressed in different ways. There are many paths, but only one abiding truth.

6. **Cosmic evolutionary optimism.** We are moving toward a glorious future of great planetary consciousness that is already beginning in this present age.

Along with these beliefs there tends to be a belief in the Eastern ideas of reincarnation (rebirth on earth in another body) and karma (the moral law that "what goes around, comes around"). These ideas provide a philosophical and spiritual undercurrent in today's world. They are part of the spiritual air that we breathe. There once was a time in our nation when Judeo-Christian tradition served as a common framework for understanding the world. In the last forty years, the philosophical worldview of Eastern religion has been gradually supplanting the Christian one. Today an eclectic mix of ideas from East and West form the matrix of popular American spirituality.

Doorways to the New Age

In a previous chapter we explored the movements and figures influential in the life and thought of Rick Warren. These same influences open the door for the introduction of New Age ideas into evangelical Christianity.

Pragmatism

Pragmatism opens the door to The New Age. The philosophical foundation of the *Purpose-Driven* model is Christian pragmatism, which says that if something works then it is good. Warren has gone even further and said that if something is working, then it is God. He looks for what is causing growth elsewhere and then adopts that method in his congregation, assured that it is has the blessing of God. This was the assumption behind the work of Donald

McGavran, Peter Wagner, and the Church Growth Movement. The test of whether something is the work of God is whether it produces growth. In *The Purpose-Driven Church* it is the numerical growth of the congregation. In *The Purpose-Driven Life* it is the spiritual growth of the individual Christian.

If the godliness of an idea or practice is measured solely by its ability to produce growth, then New Age ideas and practices are acceptable for the Christian if they work. The Unitarian Universalist Association is the only one of the old mainline denominations that is experiencing growth because they have openly welcomed New Age teachings and practices. We see this same pragmatic reasoning articulated by Robert Schuller. In his introduction to Paul Yonggi Cho's book, *The Fourth Dimension*, Schuller endorses the New Age visualization techniques contained in the book. Schuller wrote: "Don't try to understand it. Just start to enjoy it! It's true. It works. I tried it."[14] Schuller's advice is to put your mental reservations aside. Just try it. If it works, then great! Enjoy the ride. In the name of "consecrated pragmatism," any spiritual practice is acceptable if it seems to work.

Religious Pluralism

Religious pluralism produces an atmosphere conducive to New Age influence. We live in an age where the greatest virtue is tolerance. No greater insult can be directed toward a person than to be called "intolerant." "Fundamentalist" has become a dirty word. Whereas it used to designate one who held to the fundamentals of historic Christianity, now it is a synonym for terrorist. To be unaccepting of other religious viewpoints is to be guilty of "hate speech" or "spiritual violence." Postmodern pluralism celebrates diversity and encourages an attitude of acceptance and cooperation. In ecumenical circles, to accuse another of not being Christian because of faulty theology is considered disruptive to Christian unity and cooperation.

Rick Warren reflected this in his *USA Today* interview when he said, "I'm not going to get into a debate over the nonessentials. I won't try to change other denominations. Why be divisive?"[15] Warren is a champion of religious pluralism. He purposely takes no part in the theological debates of his denomination, and he will not get involved in the political battles of conservative Christians. He sees all of these activities as disruptors of unity and distractions from the goal of church growth.

This posture of neutrality fosters the attitude that theological and moral issues are nonessential and unimportant. They are matters of personal preference, like choosing between different flavors of ice cream. This tacit acceptance of variety in religious expression is the pulse of popular American spirituality. It is the spirit of the age, and Rick Warren has embraced this spirit.

Recently I received the quarterly alumni publication from my undergraduate alma mater, a historically Baptist school that long ago shed its Christian identity. The topic of the issue was "Spirit," which meant religious expression on campus. It was a celebration of spiritual correctness, the unequivocal endorsement of every form of religious expression from spiritualism to agnosticism. One "unaffiliated" student summed up the ecumenical spirit of the campus, "'I haven't found one religion that's appealed to me personally,' she says, adding that almost every religion she experiences has something in it that she likes. 'As of now I don't choose to affiliate myself with any one tradition, although Buddhism is the one I relate to the most,' she says. 'I enjoy the buffet approach to religion.'"[16]

The Purpose-Driven Life caters to this buffet approach to religion. There are no warnings from the author that most foods on the American spiritual smorgasbord are poisonous. The impression is that it is perfectly acceptable to sample whatever you want. After all, you are the spiritual consumer, and the customer is always right!

Theological Ambiguity

Theological ambiguity also makes megachurch Christians much more vulnerable to New Age spirituality. As we have already seen, Rick Warren's Saddleback Church relegates theology to the backwaters of church life. Precision in doctrine is considered divisive. To be too exact in spelling out what is theologically acceptable would drastically reduce the number of people willing to join Saddleback Church. Therefore Christian doctrine is described in the broadest possible terms. Rather than getting into the messy business of trying to define God, Saddleback's one sentence statement says simply: "God is bigger and better and closer than we can imagine."[17] Instead of wrestling with the divinity and humanity of Christ, or saying anything about his birth, death, or resurrection, Saddleback just says: "Jesus is God showing himself to us."[18] *The Purpose-Driven Life* has a "big tent" theology that can include many creeds under its flaps. Such theological diversity lays down a red carpet for those with aberrant theology to gain a hearing.

When I was the pastor of a Baptist church in Lowell, Massachusetts, the local ministerial organization was planning a citywide ecumenical Pentecost service. A local Christian Science church wanted to join the celebration. Coming from a family of Christian Science readers, I had studied the religion in depth. I knew it to be nothing more than Eastern philosophy translated into Christian vocabulary. I stridently objected to including a cultic group in a Christian service.

My objection was overruled, and I left that ecumenical organization. The other ministers in the town saw nothing unchristian about Christian Science. This same mindset is rampant in evangelical ecumenism today. Theological differences are seen as unimportant. All that matters is a sense of Christian unity and love. With an attitude of Christian acceptance and tolerance, megachurches have opened their doors to New Age beliefs and practices.

Guilt By Association

When reading *The Purpose-Driven* Life, you don't get the impression that it is a New Age textbook. Indeed, to the theologically untrained eye, it appears solidly evangelical. But upon closer examination, the pop spirituality connections are apparent. Warren Smith, former follower of the New Age movement, has written a book entitled, *Deceived On Purpose: The New Age Implications of the Purpose-Driven Church.*[19] With exhaustive documentation, Smith details the influence of New Age figures and ideas in Rick Warren's book.

The reason it is so difficult for the average reader to identify the New Age connection in the American megachurch is because of the ambiguous nature of the New Age itself. It is not an organized religion; it is a loose network of philosophies, psychologies, and spiritualities that share an occult heritage and an Eastern religious worldview. Twenty years ago, Douglas Groothuis wrote: "Whether from Eastern religions, the occult, the new psychologies, the 'frontier' theories of science, New Age politics, or New Age versions of Christianity, various ideas with a common theme are converging on our culture, pressing their way to the philosophical and ideological center of society."[20] Groothuis' prophecy has come true. New Age assumptions and ideas are very much a part of the American spiritual landscape. Whereas the biblical worldview used to be "the philosophical and ideological center of society" in America, today New Age ideas are part of the common wisdom of our culture.

Robert Schuller

In a section entitled "Laying the Groundwork: New Age Preacher Norman Vincent Peale," Rick Warren's biographer clearly describes Peale's teachings as the foundation of *The Purpose-Driven Life*.[21] Peale's teachings came to Warren through Peale's disciple, Robert Schuller. The worldview of *The Purpose-Driven Life* is soaked in Schuller's "possibility thinking." After careful comparison of the writings of the two men, Warren Smith observes that many of Warren's ideas and terms come directly from Robert Schuller's books.[22] The two men's beliefs are so similar that Smith concludes that one of Warren's purposes in writing the book was to translate Schuller's teachings into language acceptable to evangelical Christianity.[23]

Robert Schuller's connections to the New Age movement are well documented, and it is through Schuller's influence that the New Age has found a hearing in evangelical Christianity. Warren Smith chronicles Schuller's close personal friendship and professional collaboration with psychiatrist Gerald Jampolsky. Jampolsky is one of the best-known proponents of the New Age cult called "A Course in Miracles." He attributes his own spiritual awakening to an encounter with Indian guru Swami Baba Muktananda. Schuller has welcomed Jampolsky as a guest on his television broadcast on more than one occasion, where he has introduced him as a fellow Christian. Crystal Cathedral has hosted "A Course in Miracles" study groups on its campus.

Bernie Siegel

Another favorite of Robert Schuller is surgeon Bernie Siegel, who is also quoted by Rick Warren in *The Purpose-Driven Life*. Known for his work with the terminally ill, Siegel has become a leader in the New Age movement. In his best-selling book, *Love, Medicine & Miracles,* Siegel tells of meeting his "inner guide," named George, who now directs his work. During a session of directed meditation, Siegel says, "I met George, a bearded, long-haired young man wearing an immaculate flowing white gown and a skullcap. It was an incredible awakening for me, because I hadn't expected anything to happen....George was spontaneous, aware of my feelings, and an excellent advisor. He gave me honest answers, some of which I didn't like at first....All I know is that he has been my invaluable companion ever since his first appearance. My life is much easier now, because he does the hard work."[24]

Bernie Siegel endorses "A Course in Miracles" and is on the board of directors of Jampolsky's *Attitudinal Healing Center*. In 1995, Robert Schuller received Bernie Siegel's endorsement on the opening page of his book, *Prayer: My Soul's Adventure With God*. Siegel wrote: "This is a beautiful book of value to all people....Robert Schuller's newest book reaches beyond religion and information to what we all need—spirituality, inspiration, and understanding. Read it and live a life with meaning."[25] Rick Warren quotes Bernie Siegel in *The Purpose-Driven Life* as one who has found the true purpose of life.[26]

Neale Donald Walsch

The most dangerous New Age books on the market today are Neale Donald Walsch's series *Conversations with God*. It is a set of automatic writings dictated to Walsch by a spirit purporting to be divine. I read the first volume, *Conversations With God: Book One,* and felt I had been in contact with a demonic voice. Someone donated a copy of it to our church library, and I could not throw it in the trash quick enough. In his 2002 book, *The New Revelations: a Conversation with God*, Walsch and his "God" praise Schuller by name and his "new reformation" based on self-esteem.[27]

One of the dominant concepts of the New Age movement is the idea of serendipity or karmic coincidence. It is the belief that every tiny event has a benevolent nature and beneficial intent. Warren Smith was seduced into the New Age movement with the repeated teaching that "there are no accidents." Seeming coincidences are seen as the work of the universe conspiring to open the individual's mind to a higher form of consciousness. Teachers appear at just the right moment. "When the student is ready, the teacher will appear" is one of the favorite sayings of the New Age movement. New Age books are presented in this light; books are believed to come to us exactly when we need them.

Walsch opens his second book saying, "This book has arrived in your life at the right and perfect time....Everything happens in perfect order, and the arrival of this book in your life is no exception."[28] Warren voices the same idea in the opening words of *The Purpose-Driven Life*: "Before you were born, God planned *this moment* in your life. It is no accident that you are holding this book."[29] Warren undoubtedly intends to communicate the Christian idea of God's providence, but ends up paraphrasing a New Age distortion of the biblical doctrine.

It is certainly true that God is in control, and that "all things work together for good...." But it is important to read the rest of the biblical verse: "to those who love God, to those who are the called according to his purpose" (Romans 8:28). Not everything that happens is a sign from God. The

Devil is also at work in the world; he prowls around like a lion seeking someone to devour (1 Peter 5:8). There are many false teachers and false teachings. Just because you happen to pick up a book, does not mean that it has God's endorsement. God expects spiritual discernment, not blind acceptance, when it comes to the literature that comes into our hands.

A New Age PEACE Plan

In 2003 Rick Warren unveiled a five-step PEACE Plan. It was his attempt to take Saddleback Church "global." According to Saddleback's website, the plan took almost two years to develop. Its purpose is to attack five global giants "holistically." Warren uses the word PEACE as an acronym for his five points. Saddleback is to lead a worldwide movement to:

- Plant churches.
- Equip servant-leaders.
- Assist the poor.
- Care for the sick.
- Educate the next generation.[30]

In an address given by Warren and his wife, Rick Warren clearly communicates that he believed that God had given him this plan.[31] What Warren did not mention is that Neale Donald Walsch received a very similar plan with the same acronym from his "God" two years earlier. In the wake of the September 11, 2001 terrorist attacks Walsch received some "new revelations" about a five-step plan to solve the global problems of war, illness, hunger, poverty, and spiritual ignorance, using the word PEACE as an acronym.

Walsch's five points share amazing similarities with Warren's. Both announce a new initiative to courageously attack the world's global problems from a spiritual perspective. Warren Smith compares the two plans and documents the use of the same words and phrases used to describe the plans. He concludes that there must be a literary connection between the two documents.[32]

When confronted in a 2005 interview with the similarities between the two PEACE plans, Warren denied having ever heard of Walsch. He laughed off the interviewer's suggestion that he could be "in cahoots with these New Agers," saying, "How funny. Nope, never met him." Warren says that the resemblance is purely superficial and coincidental, "Well, I'm sure you can find a hundred peace plans."[33] The sympathetic interviewer did not pursue the striking similarities between the two plans in timing, content, and language. This is understandable considering that the interviewer is a friend and former associate at Saddleback Church whose avowed purpose was to defend the reputation of Rick Warren.[34]

Though Rick Warren professes ignorance of Walsch, both men were contributing authors to an ecumenical anthology presenting spiritual perspectives on the September 11 terrorist attack. The book, entitled *From the Ashes: A Spiritual Response to the Attack on America,* included articles from a variety of religious leaders from Bill Hybels and T.D. Jakes to the Dalai Lama and Starhawk the witch.[35]

Walsch's New Age PEACE Plan has been very widely circulated. It was advocated by *The Global Renaissance Alliance* consisting of New Age celebrities such as Marianne Williamson and Wayne Dyer. It was showcased on the *Oprah Winfrey Show.* It was described in a PBS special entitled "There's a Spiritual Solution to Every Problem."[36] That someone as knowledgeable about the spiritual climate of America as Rick Warren could have spent two years researching and developing a Christian PEACE Plan without stumbling across this well-known New Age PEACE Plan is difficult to imagine.

Rick Warren has no hidden agenda to take evangelical Christianity into the New Age movement. Pastor Warren is not a mole for a New Age conspiracy, burrowing deep into the heart of Christianity with the intention of subverting it from within. He is a sincere and good man with the best of Christian intentions. But his willingness to borrow uncritically from popular non-Christian spiritual culture makes it easier for those with less benign intentions to subvert his movement.

Walsch is certainly trying to do exactly this. He uses the language and ideas of *The Purpose-Driven Life* as a framework to communicate his occult teachings. Walsch conducts a regular spiritual retreat based on Warren's ideas, entitled *Living Your Purpose in Today's Turbulent World. According to the Conversations With God Foundation*, "This retreat will teach you how to: Identify your purpose and create a clear mission statement right in the midst of these challenging and tumultuous times....Design a life that expresses Who You Really Are, serves other people and supports you to become the change you wish to see in the world. Identify limiting beliefs and create new beliefs that will support your purpose."[37] Neale Donald Walsch is *Purpose-Driven!*

God Has No Grandchurches

You have heard the expression, "God has no grandchildren." It is also true that God has no grandchurches or stepchurches. The church is always one generation away from extinction. The megachurches of today tend to be genuinely Christian, even though they are light on doctrine, ignorant of religious history, and tolerant of theological error, as long as the person has "accepted Jesus Christ." This is because the present megachurch leadership grew up in traditional evangelical churches. The next crop of leaders will not have the foundation of a solid theological and religious upbringing. It is this second generation of megachurch Christians who are in the most danger of influence from pop spirituality and the New Age teachings. Without an anchor for their faith, these second-generation members will be "children, tossed to and fro and carried about with every wind of doctrine, by the trickery of men, in the cunning craftiness of deceitful plotting..." (Ephesians 4:14).

Rick Warren may have no sinister purpose when it comes to the New Age, but he is naïve when it comes to the "wiles of the Devil." Warren comes out of the "positive thinking" school of Norman Vincent Peale and Robert Schuller. He is so certain of his own good intentions and so positive that God is working through him, that he cannot see the dangers. For Peale and Schuller, to allow doubts to creep into one's thoughts is sin. Negative thinking is considered detrimental to growth and hinders success. Warren's mind is so conditioned by "possibility thinking" that he has expelled from his circle of advisors anyone who disagrees with this views.

This makes him blind to the dangers facing his church. He sees no risk in his concessions to pop spirituality. The strategy of positive thinking has been so successful for him that he can't believe that the Devil really stands a chance against the good intentions of his Global PEACE Plan. He cannot imagine that his ministry could be subverted to antichristian ends. But that is precisely the adversary's plan.

Warren Smith says of his reading of *The Purpose-Driven Life*, "It didn't take long to see that Rick Warren wasn't the only one who had definite purposes for the Purpose-Driven Church. It became very clear that our spiritual adversary had his purposes, too."[38] Satan has big plans for the mainstream

American spirituality. He delights in using churches to derail the work of Christ. He would love to use Saddleback Church. Warren Smith believes he is doing that now.[39]

Pantheism With a Purpose

While speaking about the omnipresence of God, Warren says that God is closer to us than we know. He explains that every place is equally close to God. Then he quotes half of Ephesians 4:6 from the New Century Version: "He rules everything and is everywhere and is in everything."[40] Warren's "bigger and better and closer" God is not just in Christian believers, but "in everything." This is the Eastern philosophy called pantheism, one of the theological mainstays of the New Age movement. Warren got the idea from Robert Schuller: "Yes, God is alive and He is in every single human being."[41] Schuller shares this belief with his friend Bernie Siegel, "God is in everyone and everything."[42]

A study of the Greek textual evidence and other English translations of Ephesians 4:6 make it clear that the apostle Paul is referring solely to the presence of the Holy Spirit in Christian believers. Warren could have chosen any other translation to make that point clear. Even if Warren had quoted the rest of the sentence in verses 4-6, the context would have made the meaning of the verse clear. But Warren wanted to make a different point—that God is present "in everything"—and he found a translation that suited his purpose.

This false teaching is permeating various aspects of evangelicalism. Eugene Petersen has incorporated it into *The Message,* Warren's favorite paraphrase of the Bible. After saying that God is "present in all" he translates the rest of Ephesians 4:6, "Everything you are and think and do is permeated with Oneness." "Oneness" is the term the

New Age movement uses for pantheism, the idea that God is *in* everything and that God *is* everything. Maitreya, one of the false christs of the New Age, teaches this doctrine. He says, "My friends, God is nearer to you than you can imagine. God is yourself. God is within you and all around you. I am All in All. My name is Oneness."[43]

Warren is aware of the New Age implications of his affirmation that God is in everything. He makes a point of distancing himself from the most radical teaching of the New Age—that man is God. He writes, "We aren't God and *never* will be. We are humans."[44] Later he reiterates the point, referring specifically to New Age philosophy, saying it is a satanic lie to state that man is divine.[45] In 1988 Warren distinguished between the idea that God is *in* everything and that God *is* everything. He affirmed the first statement while rejecting the second.[46] Though he refutes the Eastern doctrine of monism—that everything, including man is divine—he nevertheless continues to assert the idea that God is in everything, quoting a mistranslation of the Bible as his justification.

Meditation With a Purpose

The Purpose-Driven Life advocates practices, as well as ideas, that are part of the ecumenical spirit of the age. Considering Warren's propensity for pragmatism, this is not surprising. One of the techniques that Warren teaches to develop a deeper spiritual life is meditation. It is significant that this is introduced in the same chapter as he teaches the doctrine of pantheism. The two go together in the New Age movement; meditation is the technique through which the "spiritual person" experiences oneness with the divine.

Warren quotes 1 Thessalonians 5:17 in *The Message*, "Pray without ceasing" and interprets this verse as an invitation to practice a form of Eastern meditation. He says that Christians have rejected this ancient practice because they have misunderstood the concept of meditation. They think it is an esoteric practice for mystics and monks. Not so, according to Warren. He says it is a spiritual exercise suitable for all Christians. It is easy to learn and can be used anywhere.[47] Warren advocates "breath prayers," the repetition of a word or a phrase. He got this idea from the "centering prayer" of modern contemplative Christianity, which in turn got it from the mantra of Hinduism. The Christian is instructed to continuously repeat a phrase in one's mind throughout the day. Warren encourages Christians to train their minds to continually repeat their chosen phrase throughout every day, until it is rooted in the heart and becomes second nature.[48]

This type of meditation is the Western form of an Eastern practice. It is the technique and the approach of Maharishi Mahesh Yogi's *Transcendental Mediation*. The official Transcendental Meditation website even appeals to American's propensity for pragmatism. It says, "Everyone can learn to practice the Transcendental Meditation technique successfully….It requires no effort or concentration, no special skills or change of lifestyle. You don't even have to believe that it works! Meditate regularly twice a day and you'll get results." [49]

Listen to Your Heart

For Rick Warren, the sure way to serve God is to follow your heart. In Day 30, Warren uses the acronym SHAPE to help remember the five factors in discerning the will of God. By identifying these principles we can discover the will of God for our lives.[50] The H in the acronym stands for heart. The key to following God, according to Warren, is "listening to your heart." According to Warren, "Your heart reveals the real you—what you truly are...."[51] Smith says that when he was a New Age devotee he was taught to listen to his heart and to follow his heart. It only succeeded in drawing him further away from God and deeper into the New Age movement.[52]

Mythologist Joseph Campbell, who was a professor at Sarah Lawrence College, became a darling of the New Age through the PBS series, "The Masks of God" with host Bill Moyers. He was an avowed follower of Buddhist philosophy, which he saw as the unifying truth behind the myths of all religions, including Christianity. His advice was "Follow your bliss," using the Eastern term "bliss" in place of the more Western term "heart." But the advice was the same: turn inward and seek the wisdom that is deep within you. Campbell advised people to "follow their passion." Warren says that passion is a synonym for heart.[53]

Although the Bible sometimes speaks of the heart positively, it is generally portrayed as contrary to the will of God. Genesis says of Noah's generation, "Then the Lord saw that the wickedness of man was great in the earth, and that every intent of the thoughts of his heart was only evil continually" (Genesis 6:5). The prophet Jeremiah says, "The heart is deceitful above all things, and desperately wicked" (Jeremiah 17:9). Jesus says, "For out of the heart proceed evil thoughts, murders, adulteries, fornications, thefts, false witness, blasphemies" (Matthew 15:19). Only when the heart is set on the heart of God is it a truthful witness. In this fashion God chose David "a man after his own heart" (1 Samuel 13:14).

In the Book of Acts a man named Simon had been a sorcerer, claiming to be "the great power of God." He left the occult, believed in Jesus and was baptized. Later Simon coveted the ability of Peter to bestow the gift of the Holy

Sprit through the laying on of hands. Peter said to him, "You have neither part nor portion in this matter, for your heart is not right in the sight of God. Repent therefore of this your wickedness, and pray God if perhaps the thought of your heart may be forgiven you. For I see that you are poisoned by bitterness and bound by iniquity" (Acts 8:21-23). Simon was a believer in Jesus who followed his heart into sin.

Nowhere will you find in Scripture the instruction to the Christian to follow his heart. The Bible tells us to "follow that which is good" (1 Thessalonians 5:15 KJV) and "follow righteousness, faith, love, peace with those who call on the Lord out of a pure heart" (2 Timothy 2:22 KJV). Jesus tells us simply, "Follow me" (Luke 9:59). Why would any Christian want to follow the unreliable voice of his heart when he can follow a perfect Lord through the instruction of his inerrant Word? Only a man like King Saul, who could no longer hear the voice of God, would dabble in occult practices in order to discern the will of God. (1 Samuel 28:6-7). The prophet Isaiah says about those who today are called channelers, "And when they say to you, 'Seek those who are mediums and wizards, who whisper and mutter,' should not a people seek their God?" (Isaiah 8:19).

The Company You Keep

"He who walks with wise men will be wise. But the companion of fools will be destroyed" (Proverbs 13:20). You can tell the character of a man by the company he keeps. You can tell the spirituality of an author by the writers he quotes. Rick Warren keeps some pretty strange company. When reading *The Purpose-Driven Life* you are bombarded with quotations from many different authors. Some are familiar Christian names: C.S. Lewis, Martin Luther, and A.W. Tozer. Others are respected historical personages, such as

Abraham Lincoln and Albert Einstein. Some are entertainers like Groucho Marx and Ethel Waters. Warren seems to have an affinity for Roman Catholics like Mother Teresa and Brother Lawrence. He even quotes Madame Guyon, a French mystic condemned by the Roman Catholic Church for heresy and imprisoned in the Bastille.

The most disturbing names in Warren's pantheon of quotable sages are those who publicly oppose the gospel of Jesus Christ. He quotes *Bertrand Russell*,[54] an atheist known for his refutation of Christianity, entitled *Why I am Not a Christian.* In that book Russell writes: "Religion is based, I think, primarily and mainly upon fear. It is partly the terror of the unknown and partly, as I have said, the wish to feel that you have a kind of elder brother who will stand by you in all your troubles and disputes. ... A good world needs knowledge, kindliness, and courage; it does not need a regretful hankering after the past or a fettering of the free intelligence by the words uttered long ago by ignorant men."[55]

At the beginning of his chapter entitled "Seeing Life From God's View," Warren quotes the solipsism of *Anaïs Nin*, "We don't see things as they are, we see them as we are."[56] Nin was a French feminist who was notorious for her sexual promiscuity, including bigamy. She authored female erotica, most notably her ten-volume *The Diary of Anaïs Nin.* He quotes *Thomas Carlyle*, the nineteenth century essayist who rejected Christianity and embraced Transcendentalism. His ideas were influential on the development of Socialism and helped to form Fascism. Adolf Hitler was reading one of Carlyle's books during his last days in 1945. In his spiritual biography, *Sartor Resartus* (published 1833–34 in *Fraser's Magazine*), Carlyle articulates his spiritual beliefs. He saw the material world as a cloak for the spiritual world. God is immanent in all things as a benevolent pantheistic deity.

Rick Warren quotes *George Bernard Shaw*, who was not only a playwright, but also a leader in the precursor to the theosophy movement, which sees God as an impersonal pantheistic force in nature. Warren quotes Shaw's celebration of theosophical beliefs, "This is the true joy of life: the being used up for a purpose recognized by yourself as a mighty one; being a force of nature instead of a feverish, selfish little clot of ailments and grievances, complaining that the world will not devote itself to making you happy."[57]

Aldous Huxley is also quoted appreciatively in *The Purpose-Driven Life*. Warren introduces Huxley's quote by saying, "Only shared experiences can help others." Then he quotes Huxley: "Experience is not what happens to you. It is what you do with what happens to you."[58] The experience that Huxley was referring to was the experience of using hallucinogenic drugs to alter his consciousness and bring him into an awareness of divine oneness. His book *Doors of Perception* was one of the classics of the drug culture of the 1960s. His *Perennial Philosophy* is considered one of the best anthologies of New Age spirituality.

Why does Rick Warren favorably quote an atheist, an author of erotica, a Fascist, a theosophist and several New Age authors in a book targeted at seekers looking for God? The book's intended audience is people who do not yet know Christ and are seeking spiritual answers to the questions of life. Doesn't he see any danger in introducing these names and writings to people in the very earliest stages of their spiritual journey?

It is hard to know what was going through Rick Warren's mind as he was choosing these authors to include in his primer of the spiritual life. It is disturbing to think that these are the type of writers that Warren reads for spiritual edification, and that he values their thoughts so highly that he would quote them to his readers. Are there not enough solid Christian authors to quote, that Warren was forced to resort to recommending these unchristian writers to the most vulnerable of spiritual seekers?

It is possible that Warren is ignorant of the beliefs and teachings of the people he quotes. He might have just gone through a book of quotations looking for interesting quotations that seemed to fit his ideas, without regard to the source. If that is the case, then it is even more disturbing that these spiritual teachers are the ones whose ideas most coincide with his own.

Rick Warren and the New Age

How are evangelicals to assess Rick Warren's affiliation with the New Age movement? It would be inaccurate to paint Rick Warren as an advocate for New Age spirituality. Yet it is clear that Warren has been influenced by its authors and ideas. He quotes them favorably and employs their concepts and symbols. The danger of a popular and influential evangelical pastor doing this cannot be overstated!

Rick Warren is a man of his age. He is an American spiritual leader who has an uncanny aptitude for presenting Christianity in a form that is acceptable to millions of Americans. He has tapped into the "spirit of the age" and employs the spiritual language of the masses. He has discovered what works to bring thousands of people into his Saddleback Church. He understands Americans and knows their needs. He knows what is important to them and what is not. He knows what makes them comfortable and uncomfortable. He has his finger on the pulse of American spirituality and can present Christianity in a form that people can hear, understand, and accept. That is his genius, and that is his downfall.

In casting his wide net as a fisher of men, Warren uses any and everything that will work. American seekers do not care if there is a little New Age mixed in with their gospel. They are used to it. They hear it on Oprah. They watch Wayne Dyer and Deepak Chopra on PBS. They may have read Bernie Siegel. The Saddleback Sams and Sallys targeted by Rick Warren are baby-boomers who went through the 1960s and 70s. They feel comfortable with the ideas of Eastern religions. They take yoga classes and send their children to karate classes.

The average American believes that all religions basically teach the same thing. They are not really interested in religious doctrine anyway. They are interested in application, something that will work in their personal lives. They want a spiritual message "with handles on it," as I heard a worship leader say recently, something they can take away and use during the week. Americans have embraced the ideal of religious tolerance and acceptance. They do not want an exclusivist religion that says, "My way or the highway." They want a form of Christianity that is fun on Sundays and useful on Mondays, and preferably not too time consuming. Their schedules are too crowded as it is. *The Purpose-Driven Life's* "40 days to spiritual maturity" is just about right.

The typical American has no problem with New Age beliefs and practices as long as they are in small doses and kept in their place. That is exactly what *The Purpose-Driven Life* provides—New Age in small doses. It is the Mary Poppins approach to spirituality. Just a spoonful of New Age helps the gospel go down. A little pop spirituality makes Christianity more palatable. The problem is that poison in small doses is deadly.

Jesus made this point on many occasions. "Beware the leaven of the Pharisees and Sadducees" (Matthew 16:6). Jesus was a Jew. He said he came not to abolish the Law but to fulfill it. He did not think the Pharisees were too strict. He advocated a righteousness that exceeded that of the scribes and Pharisees. He did not think the temple was obsolete. He regularly attended the Jewish festivals and called the Jerusalem temple "my Father's house." It was his zeal for the temple, which exceeded the zeal of the priests, which was his undoing. He shared many of the beliefs and practices of his brothers, the Pharisees and Sadducees. But the differences between them were crucial. He called it leaven. "'Beware of the leaven of the Pharisees and Sadducees.' Then [his disciples] understood that he did not tell them to beware of the leaven of bread, but of the doctrine of the Pharisees and Sadducees" (Matthew 16:11-12). Bad doctrine in small doses is spiritually deadly.

The apostle Paul says, "Do you not know that a little leaven leavens the whole lump? Therefore purge out the old leaven, that you may be a new lump, since you truly are unleavened" (1 Corinthians 5:6-7). A little bit of New Age teaching leavens the whole *Purpose-Driven Life*. A sprinkling of quotations from New Age thinkers changes the nature of the whole message. Many evangelicals do not want to "throw the baby out with the bathwater" by rejecting *The Purpose-Driven Life* just because it quotes occult leaders and has a few erroneous teachings. They say there is too much good in the book to reject it entirely. "Just take the good and leave the bad," they say. The Bible says: "Do you not know that a little leaven leavens the whole lump?"

You cannot take the New Age out of *The Purpose-Driven Life* any easier than you can take yeast out of bread. It is the mixture of Christian and pop spirituality in *The Purpose-Driven Life* that produces its phenomenal results. If you take the spiritual pragmatism out of Warren's book, you have removed its *modus operandi*. The buffet approach to spirituality is what makes *The Purpose-Driven Life* so attractive to seekers. The downplaying of doctrine and the elevation of practical application is what lures people. The emphasis on fulfilling the psychological needs of the seeker by blending Christianity with psychology is what makes the Saddleback gospel so successful. The religious eclecticism of *The Purpose-Driven Life* is the problem.

Warren has synthesized a new gospel for a new age. It uses the language of evangelical Christianity. It speaks of the importance of evangelism and missions in language that can stir the hearts of sincere Christian believers. His success in church growth attracts pastors tired of struggling with declining congregations and deficit budgets. But there is something wrong with Purpose-Driven spirituality. It is not the feel of the worship service, the style of music, the clothing, or the techniques. It is not how the gospel is presented; it is the nature of the gospel that is presented. There is leaven in the lump.

CHAPTER SIX

RECOVERING THE EVANGELICAL ESSENTIALS

The megachurch is too small. Rick Warren's vision of the Christian life is too limited. There is so much more to Christianity than *The Purpose-Driven Life*. What is needed is not a "New Reformation" but a return to the truths of the first Reformation. What is needed is not reformation, but recovery of the basics of evangelical Christianity. Warren's vision for the future would only bring us further down the same road that evangelicalism has been traveling for the last thirty years. These decades have been years of growth in numbers and social influence, but they have also been years of decline in theological thinking, personal morality, and mature spirituality.

There are "deep flaws in contemporary evangelical faith," says David Wells of Gordon-Conwell Theological Seminary. "It is hard to miss in the evangelical world—in the vacuous worship that is so prevalent, for example, in the shift from God to the self as the central focus of faith, in the psychologized preaching that follows this shift, in the erosion of its conviction, in its strident pragmatism, in its

173

inability to think incisively about the culture, in its reveling in the irrational."[1] This book is an attempt to expose those flaws in the writings of Rick Warren.

But, as Ecclesiastes says, there is "a time to break down, and a time to build up" (Ecclesiastes 3:3). If we only criticized *The Purpose-Driven Life*, this book would be nothing but an exercise in negativity. Evangelical Christianity is in a state of disrepair, and it is time to rebuild the walls. There are *four evangelical essentials* that need to be recovered.

The Recovery of Biblical Evangelism

First, there is a need for evangelicalism to reclaim its heritage as an evangelistic religion. Evangelism is the core of what it means to be evangelical. People who are not conversant in Christian terminology will often confuse the two terms. They will say *evangelical,* but they mean *evangelistic*—the intention to win converts. The two terms are intertwined. We do not need more psychological techniques and sociological tools to produce organizational growth. We need to recover authentic biblical evangelism.

Passion for Evangelism

Evangelicals need to recover a *passion for evangelism.* This is Rick Warren's strong suit. This is why *The Purpose-Driven Church* and *The Purpose-Driven Life* resonate with evangelical pastors. Warren has a passion for evangelism, and he communicates that passion to his readers. He inherited this enthusiasm from his Baptist forefathers and especially from his father, Jimmy Warren. The scene in *The Purpose-Driven Life* where Warren describes his father's deathbed commission to "Save one more for Jesus!" is the most moving passage in the book. He has fulfilled his promise to his father to make that the theme of the rest of his life.[2]

Rick Warren has a passion for evangelism. This factor is one of the main reasons why Saddleback Church is so successful. He has communicated his zeal to countless other pastors through his workshops and seminars. The evangelical church needs the evangelistic fervor of Rick Warren. Evangelicalism is becoming sidelined with other pursuits. A perusal of the programs that dominate Christian radio will reveal the divided heart of evangelical Christianity.

Political and social issues are high on the list of evangelical priorities. The *Moral Majority*, the *Christian Coalition* and the other incarnations of the religious right have hijacked the energy of evangelicals and put it to the service of lesser goals. Christ's kingdom is not of this world. Evangelicals need to resist the temptation to mold American society into their image. We need to return to our primary vision of bringing people to Christ. Jesus did not call us to install worldly leaders, pass better laws, or install judges sympathetic to our Christian values. He called us to spread the gospel to all nations.

The Goal of Evangelism

Evangelicals need to recover the *goal of evangelism*. Rick Warren has zeal to win souls, but it is zeal without knowledge. The apostle Paul says of his passionate Jewish brothers, "I bear them witness that they have a zeal for God, but not according to knowledge" (Romans 10:2). The passion of Rick Warren for evangelism impresses me deeply. He has found a way to harness that fervor to a method that produces thousands of converts. Furthermore, he communicates his passion using the traditional language of Christianity. This is what makes his *Purpose-Driven* model so attractive to evangelicals. But the evangelistic zeal of the Jehovah's Witnesses also impresses me. The commitment of young Mormon missionaries puts me to shame. These homegrown sects are among the fastest-growing religions in the world! I admire their zeal, but they are not bringing people into a saving relationship with Jesus Christ.

The Purpose-Driven Life falls short in its understanding of conversion. In his zeal to "win one more for Jesus" Warren has streamlined the process of conversion. Warren invites people to receive Jesus as Savior without first explaining the person and work of Jesus. He omits indispensable elements, such as confession and repentance. He reduces conversion to the formula: "receive and believe." He condenses conversion to a commitment to an undefined Jesus through the recitation of a simple prayer followed by the assurance of eternal security.

It is superficial conversion at best; at worst it is counterfeit conversion. Instead of serving as midwife at the rebirth of souls, he brings forth stillbirths. At best his program facilitates premature births that will need years of incubation to produce healthy disciples. One evangelist observes of this form of easy evangelism, "They do, however, sometimes speed the process of evangelism, making it easier to get 'commitments.' Also, they often stir up less opposition and appear to get results. However, if the 'converts' end up backsliding or falling away, of what benefit is the supposed conversion?"[3]

Evangelical Christianity needs to recover genuine conversion as described in the Bible. I call it *deep conversion* to distinguish it from the shallow salvation formula of *The Purpose-Driven Life*. The goal of evangelism is the redemption of the person, not just a change in mental and emotional allegiance. For deep conversion to occur, there needs to be spiritual surgery conducted by the Great Physician. The Holy Spirit brings a person to conviction of sin by way of godly sorrow and genuine repentance. Repentance is more than a change of mind. It is a heart transplant. The heart of stone is replaced with a heart of flesh. There is confession of sin, turning away from a life of sin, and turning toward God. These elements are missing from the *Purpose-Driven* understanding of conversion, and they need to be reclaimed.

A Theology of Evangelism

Evangelicals need to recover a *theology of evangelism*. Rick Warren has a well-developed *psychology* of evangelism based on the felt needs of the seeker. He has a *philosophy* of evangelism based in pragmatism, and he has a *methodology* of evangelism grounded in marketing techniques. But he lacks a *theology* of evangelism.

Evangelistic theology needs to be based on foundational biblical concepts. *The Purpose-Driven Life* lacks any description of *how* we are saved by God. The cross of Jesus needs to reclaim its central place in evangelical preaching. The most curious thing about the theology of *The Purpose-Driven Life* is the downplaying of the atoning work of Jesus. It is barely mentioned and never explained. Historically, the death and resurrection of Jesus played central roles in the message of evangelicalism. Today they have been replaced with a focus on the self and the practical everyday problems of life. The spotlight needs to return to the work of God in Jesus on the cross, and to his resurrection from the grave.

There likewise needs to be a focus on the grace of God working in the soul of man. Warren's view of salvation and sanctification makes it sound like a cooperative venture between a loving God and a willing heart. It flirts with, if not actually embraces, a form of Arminian theology that repeats the error of Semi-Pelagianism. The work of deep conversion is an act of divine grace in the unwilling soul of sinful man. Grace finds the lost, brings the dead to life and causes the blind to see. Conversion is not the result of seekers finding the fulfillment of their felt needs in a commitment to an undefined God. The theology behind *Purpose-Driven* evangelism is too vague and human-centered. There needs to be a return to a Christ-centered theology of salvation.

A Commitment to Evangelism

Evangelicals need to recover a *commitment to evangelism*. Bill Bright said that only two percent of American Christians share their faith with others.[4] This reveals our lack of commitment to personal evangelism. Once again, we can give Rick Warren a round of applause for returning the attention of evangelicals back to the task of evangelism. In too much of evangelicalism, it has been business as usual for many years.

Most evangelical churches do not make evangelism a top priority in the life of the congregation. Take a look at any church budget and you can get a snapshot of the priorities of the congregation. In the typical church, about forty percent goes to the building and facilities. Another forty percent goes to administration, including office expenses and salary packages. Ten percent goes to missions. The remaining ten percent covers all the programming of the church including education, worship, social ministries, and—if there is anything left over—evangelism.

The priorities of a congregation can also be assessed by how its members use their time. Once again, evangelism is low in the evangelical pecking order. Worship, meetings, administration, maintenance, and educational programming take up the majority of the schedule in the typical church. Most activities of the average church are directed inward to the congregation. That which is directed outward is usually in the form of social ministry.

Barna's research reveals "Protestant pastors work an average of nearly sixty-five hours per week, juggling sixteen major dimensions of activity."[5] Most of that time is taken up with preparation for preaching, teaching, worship, visitation, and administration. Most pastoral visitation is with those who are already members of the congregation. The remainder is with nonmembers who have attended a worship service. Evangelistic efforts by the pastor are centered on the regular worship service or special church programs. These outreach programs are efforts to invite outsiders to come into the church where they can hear the gospel. The focus remains inward. Very little time, money, or energy is directed beyond the church walls.

Jesus did not invite people to come into the temple or the synagogue. He told his disciples to go out. The Great Commission of Christian evangelism says: "*Go* therefore and make disciples of all nations..." (Matthew 28:18). The church building is not the setting for evangelism. It is the place where people are inspired and equipped to go out and do evangelism. Evangelism happens outside the church walls. It happens in the world where people live. One of the reasons new churches grow, while old churches dwindle, is because newly planted congregations have no buildings. They are forced to go out into the world, meeting in hotel ballrooms and school auditoriums. The evangelistic church is *in the world* where it can be a light *to the world*, rather than under a bushel where their light is covered.

If evangelical churches are to recover their evangelistic focus, they will need to make a commitment to evangelism. That commitment will be measured in hours and dollars, dedicating more of the church's time, energy, and resources to the work of evangelism. It may mean getting rid of the church building and going to where the unchurched are. It will mean dedicating at least as much money to local evangelistic efforts as it gives to foreign missions. Evangelistic missions, like charity, begin at home.

It will mean designating more of the pastor's time to minister to those who are not members of the congregation, even if that means that the felt needs of the church members will have to be met by lay ministry. The pastor is instructed in the Bible to "do the work of an evangelist," but the truth is there is little time or energy to do such work. The pastor will have to make a commitment to preach about evangelism. The educational program will have to instruct its members in evangelism. The congregation will have to fund evangelism. Christians will have to practice evangelism. Evangelism will have to become a lifestyle rather than something church members pay professional clergy to do on their behalf.

Leadership is indispensable when it comes to reorganizing a church to make evangelism a priority. Making a commitment to evangelism may mean calling a minister of evangelism. Usually when a church contemplates adding another staff position, it is a youth pastor, minister of music, or an associate pastor with a broad portfolio of responsibilities. But if a church calls a minister of evangelism, then the position will pay for itself in a few years. If the minister is gifted in the area of evangelism, then the fruit of his ministry will bring a harvest of people into the church who will pay for his salary, thereby freeing up monies for other staff positions. First there has to be the commitment to take a step of faith and reorient the life of the church to do the work of evangelism.

Tools For Evangelism

Evangelicals need to use modern *tools for evangelism*. This is another area where Rick Warren can help us. The social sciences must not drive the church's agenda, but nei-

180

ther must they be neglected. Evangelicalism has long had an unhealthy attitude toward science..The influence of fundamentalism has left evangelicalism with an antiscientific bias. The megachurches have erred in the opposite direction, embracing indiscriminately the philosophy and conclusions of science. If the church is to recover its evangelistic focus, it must use sociological tools without being controlled by the secular worldview that often accompanies them.

Demographic data and community surveys can help a congregation understand its neighborhood without letting the felt needs of the neighborhood determine its message. Technology has long been used by evangelicals, and rightly so. Churches need to use the best possible tools to communicate the message. Even marketing strategies can aid a congregation in clearly presenting the gospel without changing the gospel to appeal to the market. All churches engage in marketing, whether or not they admit it. It is simply a matter of who is in control—the consumer or Christ. Evangelical Christians must be wise as serpents and innocent as doves. Unfortunately, the serpents have been devouring the doves in the megachurches. The evangelical congregation needs to be retooled for the twenty-first century if it is to recover its historic emphasis on evangelism.

The Recovery of Evangelical Theology

Second, there is a need to reclaim evangelical theology. Mark Noll of Wheaton College has written a scathing indictment of evangelicalism for its dearth of intellectual pursuits. He begins the book, "The scandal of the evangelical mind is that there is not much of an evangelical mind....Notwithstanding all their other virtues, however, American evangelicals are not exemplary for their thinking, and they have not been for several generations."[6] Somewhere during the twentieth century, doctrine was deemed of little importance.

Rick Warren stands in a long line of seminary-trained evangelicals who have exchanged the theological enterprise for success measured in church attendance, income, and prestige. Seminary professor, David Wells, laments the loss. "The new quest for contemporary practicality has transformed the nature of the Christian ministry, the work of the seminaries, and the inner workings in denominational headquarters, and in each case the transformation has sounded the death knell of theology ... Seminary students are not blind to the fact that the big churches and the big salaries go to those who are untheological or even anti-theological."[7]

Warren has followed in this tradition of pastors as managers rather than theologians. The result of this anti-theological bias is a deterioration of the quality of theology in the evangelical church. If theology is not important, then it really does not matter what you believe. Theology is equated with religion; the megachurch sees itself as above the petty doctrinal squabbles of religion. Evangelicals repeat the phrase like a mantra: Christianity is not a religion. Theological and philosophical reflection on the truths of the Bible is pushed aside in favor of more practical considerations.

Therefore the quality of evangelical doctrine suffers. Compromises are made with worldly philosophies. Growth becomes more important than faithfulness to the theological truths of the Bible. Doctrinal differences are viewed as divisive, hindering the unity needed to accomplish church goals. Cooperative ventures with other religions require a downplaying of theological differences. Theological statements are reduced to "lowest common denominator" documents that can accommodate a vast number of theological interpretations.

In *The Scandal of the Evangelical Conscience*, Ron Sider relates a disturbing trend discerned by an evangelical pastor. For six years the pastor taught a class for teenagers entering the membership of his congregation. He placed a jar of marbles before them and asked them how many marbles were in the jar. They responded with different guesses. The pastor informed them that there were exactly 157 marbles. "The quantity of marbles is a matter of fact, not personal opinion," he observed. Then he asked the group their favorite songs. After they shared the names of the tunes they liked best, he asked them which song was the right answer. They replied that there was no "right song." It was a matter of musical taste and personal opinion. The pastor agreed.

The pastor then instructed them in some of the essential doctrines of Christianity, including the deity of Christ and the resurrection of Jesus from the grave. He explained to them that some people do not believe these things. He then asked them, "Are the deity of Jesus Christ and his resurrection matters of fact, or are they matters of personal opinion? Are they like the question of the number of marbles in the jar, or like the question of which music you prefer?" Every one of the students for six years said that the deity and resurrection of Christ are like music—a matter of personal opinion! [8]

This is the theological legacy of evangelicalism. Doctrine is a matter of personal opinion. In small group discussions, no one's opinion is labeled wrong. That would be judgmental and detrimental to the fellowship of the group, as well as lowering the person's self-esteem! The downplaying of doctrine has produced religious relativism. Consequently, theology is relegated to a back page of the Saddleback website. The doctrinal statement that is presented is so broad that it can include any heresy you can imagine.

Recovery of Theological Passion

The recovery of theology in evangelical churches must start with a *passion for theology*. Theology must be seen as central to the spiritual life of the congregation. It has to be viewed as more important than what people feel they need. It has to be more important than church growth. Theology precedes evangelism. If the church's theology is not sound, then there is no gospel to preach! It has to be understood as more important than budgets. If the truth is not preached from the pulpit, what does it matter how much money is in the treasury?

Theology has to be seen as more important than life itself. Martin Luther laid his life on the line for biblical theology at the Diet of Worms. When commanded to renounce the truths of the gospel in favor of preserving church unity and his own life, he said, *"My conscience is captive to the Word of God. I cannot and I will not recant anything for to go against conscience is neither right nor safe. God help me. Amen."* This was the decisive moment of the Protestant Reformation. Today the theological differences between Catholics and Protestants are downplayed. History is being rewritten by the ecumenically tolerant. The Reformation is increasingly seen as a mistake. The ecumenical document *Evangelicals and Catholics Together* glosses over theological differences in order to present a united front against what are seen as common foes. There needs to be a passion for theological truth that is strong enough to confront the evangelical tendency toward theological compromise in the name of ecumenical unity.

Recovery of Theological Basics

Because theology has been neglected for so long, there has arisen a generation that is ignorant of the basic truths of Christianity. There needs to be a return to an affirmation of the doctrinal essentials of the faith. Fundamentalism tried to do that in the early twentieth century with the seven "fundamentals" of the faith. That has proven to be too limited a definition of Christianity. Instead we need to return to the basics of Reformation theology.

A good place for a congregation to begin would be a study of the five *solas* of the Reformation. *The Cambridge Declaration* of the Alliance of Confessing Evangelicals is a document signed by fourteen evangelical leaders in 1996 as an attempt to return evangelicals to theological integrity grounded in Reformation truths. Truth is determined solely on the authority of Scripture (*sola scriptura*). Salvation is by grace alone (*sola gratia*) through faith alone (*sola fide*) in Christ alone (*solus Christus*) to the glory of God alone (*soli Deo gloria*).[9]

In order to recover theological integrity in evangelical churches, there needs to be a return to the practice of articulating theology in doctrinal statements. Baptists, like Rick Warren, have historically been a non-creedal people. Instead of pledging allegiance to authoritative creeds that bear the marks of sinful man, Baptists have advocated *confessions of faith*.[10] These theological documents are descriptive of Baptist beliefs while not compromising the sole authority of Scripture. Historically, both congregations and associations have adopted confessions of faith as a way of keeping theology preeminent in Christian identity.

Recovery of Theological Education

One tool used by evangelicals to educate their congregations on biblical doctrine has been the *catechism*. Based on the *confessions of faith*, a *catechism* is a way of communicating the essentials of biblical truth to new converts. Today's "new member classes" in most churches tend to be no more than a brief introduction to church life. Sider says, "We almost certainly would strengthen the church today if we made it harder to join. For much of the first three centuries, new converts went through an extensive teaching process, finally experiencing baptism on Easter Sunday." He notes early Anabaptists and Wesleyans as examples, "In both instances…there was no hurry in taking someone into membership. Tests of membership included behavior as well as doctrine."[11]

Warren, on the other hand, advocates immediate baptism, citing the Ethiopian eunuch as the biblical model. He says that the sole biblical condition for baptism is faith. He insists that there are no delayed baptisms in the Bible and there should be none in the church today. He urges his readers who prayed the little prayer of chapter seven to be baptized as quickly as possible.[12] This practice produces impressive numbers in the church reports, but it also produces theologically-ignorant church members.

Theological education needs to be taken seriously in evangelical churches. Saddleback Church has classes on theology. In his chapter on "Developing Mature Members" Warren describes Saddleback's "Life Perspectives I" class. He says it is his church's systematic theology course. It was written by his wife, Kay, along with Saddleback's pastor of Spiritual Maturity, Tom Holladay.[13] Systematic theology written by the pastor's wife! Unless Mrs. Warren is also a seminary theology professor, this is inappropriate. It communicates a cavalier attitude concerning the importance of the subject. Warren insists on hiring professional musicians for his church's music program because he sees it as important. Why not call in a professional theologian to write and teach Saddleback's theology course? A church the size of Saddleback could hire a faculty of seminary professors! Theology needs to be taken seriously in evangelical churches.

Sunday school should be more than Bible stories for children, Bible games for youth, and practical application of biblical principles for adults. There needs to be instruction in doctrine. Evangelical churches have shied away from doctrinal instruction so as not to be accused of *indoctrination*. The word *indoctrination* has become a dirty word in today's culture. It carries connotations of brainwashing. But the word means simply to "instruct in a body of doctrine." It is the responsibility of the church to instruct its members in the eternal truths of God's Word so that they will think correctly. The word *orthodox* means, "to think straight." To neglect the task of communicating orthodoxy is to invite heresy—another dirty word these days. Neglecting theological education is acquiescing to theological relativism, which undercuts the gospel by saying that truth is just a matter of personal opinion.

Recovery of Theological Preaching

The pastor is the primary teacher of theology in the church. The apostle Paul says he was appointed by God as a preacher, an apostle and "a teacher of the Gentiles in faith and truth." One of Paul's qualifications for pastors is that they must be "able to teach" (1 Timothy 3:2). He tells the young pastor Timothy to charge those under his authority to "teach no other doctrine" than that which Paul had passed on (1 Timothy 1:3). He says, "If you instruct the brethren in these things, you will be a good minister of Jesus Christ, nourished in the words of faith and of the good doctrine which you have carefully followed" (1 Timothy 4:6). Part of the pastor's task is to pass on sound doctrine to those who can teach it faithfully. "And the things that you have heard from me among many witnesses, commit these to faithful men who will be able to teach others also" (2 Timothy 2:2).

The pastor cannot avoid responsibility to teach theology in the church. One of the chief ways that he fulfills this commission is in the sermon. There is a need to recover theological preaching. It is the opinion of megachurch pastors that people will not stand for doctrinal preaching. They may be right. The Bible says, "For the time will come when they will not endure sound doctrine, but according to their own desires, because they have itching ears, they will heap up for themselves teachers; and they will turn their ears away from the truth, and be turned aside to fables" (2 Timothy 4:3-4).

Preachers give their congregations whatever keeps them happy; otherwise they will just go to another church down the street. They entertain their congregation with anecdotes, illustrations, and personal testimonies. These are the modern equivalents of the "old wives tales" and "cleverly devised fables" of ancient times (1 Timothy 4:7; 2 Peter 1:16). The pastor is supposed to "shun profane and idle babblings for they will increase to more ungodliness" (2 Timothy 2:16). Paul exhorts pastors, "Preach the Word! Be ready in season and out of season. Convince, rebuke, exhort, with all longsuffering and teaching" (2 Timothy 4:2).

The pastor has the responsibility to teach sound doctrine. It is a serious responsibility and needs to be taken seriously. James says, "My brethren, let not many of you become teachers, knowing that we shall receive greater judgment" (James 3:1). If we neglect our responsibility, the fate of souls shall be upon our heads. God made the prophet Ezekiel "a watchman for the house of Israel." He told him, "Therefore hear a word from My mouth, and give them warning from Me." He goes on to explain the consequences of this ministry: "When I say to the wicked, 'You shall surely die.' And you give him no warning, nor speak to warn the wicked from his wicked way, to save his life, that same wicked man shall die in his iniquity; but his blood I will require at your hand" (Ezekiel 3:17-18).

Paul instructed Timothy, concerning those who have "strayed from the truth," "Remind them of these things, charging them before the Lord not to strive about words to no profit, to the ruin of the hearers. Be diligent to present yourself approved to God, a worker who does not need to be ashamed, rightly dividing the word of truth" (2 Timothy 2:14-15). The pastor has a solemn responsibility before God to preach sound doctrine. This will necessitate more than an annual sermon on Reformation Sunday. It will mean series of messages on theological themes such as the doctrine of God, the doctrine of Christ, and the Atonement. A sermon series on the biblical doctrine of creation would go a long way in correcting the tunnel vision of the evolution-creationism debate!

Pastors need to go beyond the "how-to" sermons that Rick Warren advocates and preach the eternal truths of the Bible, regardless of whether they can be applied directly to the problem *du jour*. Ultimately even what appears to be the most theoretical theological truth will be revealed as practical in the long run. When "the whole counsel of God" is systematically proclaimed so as to produce a coherent biblical worldview in the mind of the Christian, then it will serve as a sure foundation to address all the problems of life. Anything less is applying Band-Aids to whatever is hurting at the moment.

Theology changes lives. It changes the way we think about God, the world, and ourselves. Give a person a "how-to" sermon, and it may work at the moment. But the next time a problem arises, the Christian will have to return to the pastor to get another fix. Change a person's worldview, and he can make his own decisions. It is the proverbial difference between giving a man a fish and teaching him to fish. Theological preaching teaches a man to think theologically. He will view life through the eyes of God. "For *who has known the mind of the Lord that he may instruct Him?* But we have the mind of Christ" (1 Corinthians 2:16).

The Recovery of Evangelical Spirituality

Tradition! *Fiddler on the Roof* can sing about it, but evangelicals cannot sing along. It is another one of those words that has been banned from evangelical religion. To the average evangelical, the word *tradition* implies all that is wrong with "organized religion." Wolfe understates the case when he talks about "the rather limited role that tradition plays in America's evangelical subculture."[14] Another expert on seeker churches writes, "Tradition, according to many pastors poses an unnecessary barrier for seekers who are trying to bridge the gap between their relatively secular daily lives and the evangelical teachings of seeker churches."[15] The banishment of the collective wisdom of the past has made evangelicalism a captive to the present, and vulnerable to the spiritual fads of the newest Christian bestseller. There is a need to recover the rich spiritual heritage of Protestant evangelicalism.

Recovery of Spiritual Disciplines

Popular evangelical spirituality does not go much beyond conversion. We dunk them and leave them to wander the world until they get to heaven. This void of spiritual resources for daily life has been filled with the spiritual practices and techniques of pop spirituality. Eastern religious practices have been imported into Christianity. Christians practice "Christian" yoga and "Christian" meditation. People are under the illusion that they are harmless exercises and relaxation techniques with no religious content. Actually, they are Hindu practices that cannot be separated from their religious roots. The whole area of Christian "contemplative prayer" has arisen to give Christians some tools to deepen their spiritual lives. Richard Foster has filled the gap with books such as his popular *The Celebration of Discipline*. There is much that is good in his books, but his Quaker heritage makes him too accepting of spiritual practices that are beyond the range of traditional Christianity.

The problem with evangelical spirituality is that we have emphasized justification and neglected sanctification. We emphasize the initial change in our relationship with God that takes place at conversion, but ignore the continuing spiritual change that must take place in our lives. Sider observes: "I am convinced that at the heart of our problem is a one-sided, unbiblical, reductionist understanding of the gospel and salvation ... Salvation becomes, not a life-transforming experience that reorients every corner of life, but a one-way ticket to heaven, and one can live like hell until one gets there."[16]

For ongoing spiritual transformation to occur, there needs to be a regular practice of spiritual disciplines. There needs to be a dedication to private prayer. There is no need for more church programs—forty days or otherwise. There is a need for more prayer. Evangelicals of previous centuries spent hours on their knees before God. Such dedication to prayer is unknown today. Today a quick "quiet time" squeezed into our schedule at the beginning or end of the day is considered an accomplishment. Many pastors neglect even that! Evangelicals do not know what to pray or how to pray. Our prayers tend to be shopping lists of healings we want God to perform or problems we want him to solve. When we come to the end of the list, we fall silent and feel embarrassed for being bored in the presence of the Almighty. The forms of biblical prayer beyond petition and intercession are neglected.

Family devotions have been traded for "quality time" before the television. Bible reading is replaced by evangelical "how-to" books on solving relationship problems. For all the evangelical talk about the Bible, we are the most biblically illiterate generation of Protestants in history. I am appalled at how many Christians have never read the whole Bible through once! Fasting is replaced by diets. Brotherly exhortation and encouragement are replaced by professional Christian counseling. There is a need to recover basic evangelical spiritual disciplines.

Recovery of Spiritual Heritage

I wonder how many Baptists in Saddleback Church, the largest Baptist Church in America, can name any people from early Baptist history. Could they tell you when and where Baptists began? Could the typical evangelical today in a church tell you the difference between a Baptist and a Jehovah's Witness—beyond the willingness of the Witnesses to engage in door-to-door evangelism? Can the average evangelical tell you why there was a Protestant Reformation?

Evangelicals have a bad case of historical amnesia. As the saying goes, if we do not know history, we will repeat it. If we do not know about the Reformation, we will have to repeat it! If we do not know the church's careful struggle to understand the nature and person of Christ as formulated in the early church councils, then we will fall into Christological error. If we do not reclaim our history, we will be doomed to reprise it.

It has been said that we live in a post-denominational world. Evangelicals are proud of being *nondenominational*, as if it were a badge of honor. It is more likely a badge of ignorance. Most people say they are nondenominational because they do not know anything about denominational distinctives, and furthermore, they do not care! Their churches have no roots, their theologies no depth, and their practices no history. Evangelical ecumenism is thriving, not because of a greater sense of unity in Christ, but because of lack of knowledge of Christ. Evangelicalism has been reduced to a personal experience of Jesus, and it doesn't really matter which Jesus it is! Sacraments are shared across denominational lines, not because evangelicals have entered into deeper Christian communion, but because they no longer know what *sacrament* means! Baptists have no sacraments. Yet I have been in a Baptist church where a deacon stood beside the communion table and thanked God for the "sacrament" of the Lord's Supper!

We do not need to return to the denominational conflicts of previous centuries. But we need to know that the theological and historical issues that gave rise to the denominations are still important. Theology matters. Church polity matters. Worship practices matter. For most evangelicals today, none of that matters. Nothing matters to Christians but their personal relationship to Jesus. Nothing matters to church leaders other than growing their church. "Early in their history, evangelicals were prepared to abandon tradition for the sake of doctrinal purity. Now they are prepared to abandon tradition for the sake of organizational growth."[17]

Recovery of Spiritual Community

We live in an age of spiritual "lone rangers." George Barna observes that one of the changes that has taken place in the evangelical church is that it is no longer a community but a pit stop. Their church is not their final destination, but just a rest stop on their spiritual journey.[18] There is no more loyalty to the local church than there is to denominational labels. Churches are nothing more than places to have our personal needs met and our personal lifestyles affirmed. If a church does not do the job well enough, we just move on to another. Peter Gillquist says, "We have become such a nation of self-lovers. Nothing is too sacred to leave—if we feel like it. We leave school if it gets boring or difficult; we leave home and parents if we're displeased; we leave our jobs, our marriages, and our churches."[19]

The church is no longer a place of spiritual community. It is a pit stop on Sunday mornings for spiritual refueling. It is ironic that the word *community* is the favorite label of megachurches. That is exactly what megachurches are not! They are anonymous cities of seekers. The cell groups that are supposed to foster a sense of interpersonal connection in these huge churches have only succeeded in being mini-churches that are exited quickly when the content or relationships do not suit a person's liking.

An integral part of spiritual community is discipline. Nothing reveals the loss of evangelical community as much as the lack of church discipline. This is a result of the consumer mentality of American spirituality. Haddon Robinson says, "Too often now when people join a church, they do so as consumers. If they like the product, they stay. If they do not, they leave. They can no more imagine a church disciplining them than they could a store that sells goods disciplining them. It is not the place of the seller to discipline the consumer."[20] In an issue of *Christianity Today* dedicated to the topic of church discipline, Marlin Jeschke says that many megachurch Christians are "church hoppers or perennial visitors, considering themselves free-floating Christians without accountability—and they like it that way." [21]

Evangelical spirituality has died because there is no accountability between members. Each member is viewed as an autonomous unit coming to the church for weekly refueling. The Bible says that we are to "exhort one another daily, while it is called 'Today,' lest any of you be hardened through the deceitfulness of sin" (Hebrews 3:13). The pastor's role is to "convince, rebuke, exhort, with all longsuffering and teaching" (2 Timothy 4:2). Concerning church leaders Paul says, "Those who are sinning rebuke in the presence of all, that the rest also may fear" (1 Timothy 5:20). One of the two times that Jesus uses the word *church* was in the context of church discipline, spelling out for us the procedure to take (Matthew 18:17).

Church discipline has been abandoned because Christian community has been lost. In its place is an attraction for Christian consumers, a refueling station at the beginning of the week. The church is now just a place to stay as long as your felt needs are being met. If something does not suit your fancy, or if your sins become so apparent that your Christian façade can no longer be maintained, then it is on to the next church. This has been referred to as the "circulation of the saints."[22] There is a need to recover an authentic sense of Christian community that befits the rhetoric of the church as the family of God.

The Recovery of Spiritual Worship

One of the greatest weaknesses of the megachurch is its worship. Paradoxically this is also its greatest attraction to the public. If the megachurch forsakes its entertainment-style Sunday morning "celebration," then it will lose its customer base. Those who are coming for the show will go elsewhere. It is unlikely that the megachurch will willingly forsake this hen that lays the golden eggs. But if evangelical Christianity is to recover its soul, it needs to do exactly this.

Evangelical Christianity needs to reclaim its symbolism. A church cannot do without symbols, regardless of the convictions of the Society of Friends! If it forsakes Christian symbols, then pagan symbols will sneak in the back door, as we have seen with the symbolism of *The Purpose-Driven Life*. The cross, which was the scandal of the first century and is still a scandal today, needs to be courageously embraced regardless of the cost. Evangelicals need to take up the cross and follow Jesus. Architecture needs to reflect the glory of God and not just the comfort of man. The sense of sacred space in the church building needs to be recovered. The church is to be holy as God is holy. The place where the saints gather needs to reflect sacredness.

The order of worship needs to include basic Christian elements. God's house has to once again become a "house of prayer." Jesus was so angry that he became violent because the temple leaders had so commercialized religion that it was no longer possible for people to pray. Evangelicals have done the same thing. Prayer has been banished from congregational worship. It needs to be restored.

There must be opportunity for prayers of confession of sin and repentance, both corporate and individual. The worship service cannot be limited to what is fun and happy. It needs to allow for godly sorrow and tears of repentance. That scary space called *silence* needs to be invited back into evangelical worship. Seekers find silence scary because God is in the silence. Silence is the holy of holies; it is the most intimate presence of God. It is where we meet God face to face, and that can be scary! It is all right to fear God! In fact we are commanded to fear God.[23] Yet, this is exactly the emotion that is choreographed out of evangelical worship!

The apostle Paul says to "work out your own salvation in fear and trembling; for it is God who works in you both to will and to do for His good pleasure" (Philippians 2:12-13). We need to give God the space to work in us instead of crowding out the Holy Spirit by manufacturing happy feelings.

The most ubiquitous symbol of American society is the yellow happy face. I recently saw a man walking a beach with a big yellow happy face tee shirt and a happy face cap. I confess that I had unhappy feelings toward him. The Devil must know my dislike for the symbol; he inspired our neighbor across the street to erect a big bulbous plastic happy face on his stockade fence facing our front porch. I planted a forsythia bush to block the sunny smile. Much of evangelical worship gives me the feeling that I am staring at a yellow round happy face.

There is more to the range of human emotions in worship than happiness. Warren says he will not play any music in a minor key because it does not communicate the "upbeat, bright, joyful" emotions he wants in worship.[24] Some of my favorite hymns are in a minor key. *Be Thou My Vision* touches a place my soul that *This is the Day* just can't reach. Christians have told me that they have stayed away from worship for weeks or months because they were sad. They were depressed, grieving, or going through hard times, and did not feel like they had the strength to put on their happy face. So they stayed away from church! That is the scandal of evangelical worship! The range of emotions acceptable for evangelical worship is too narrow. The understanding of worship is too small. We need to recover the full spiritual range of evangelical worship.

The Recovery of Evangelical Ethics

Evangelicals are not known for their morals. "Gallup and Barna hand us survey after survey demonstrating that evangelical Christians are as likely to embrace lifestyles every bit as hedonistic, materialistic, self-centered, and sexually immoral as the world in general."[25] The ethical behavior of evangelicalism is appalling. Christians have acquiesced to the same worldliness as their non-Christian neighbors. In every category Christians act and think no differently than anyone else. Evangelicals need to recover a sense of the importance of living an ethical lifestyle that glorifies God. Presently we are more interested in fulfilling our own needs, and the megachurch encourages us in our worldliness.

The Bible clearly says that where there is no godly living, there is no faith in God. Evangelical faith unaccompanied by ethical living is a lifeless imitation of Christianity. The apostle James says, "Thus also faith by itself, if it does not have works is dead" (James 2:17). "For as the body without the spirit is dead, so faith without works is dead also" (James 2:26). The evangelical distortion of the doctrine of *justification by faith alone* has caused us to downplay the role of works in the Christian life. The Bible makes it clear that there is no faith without works. No new birth has occurred if there is no accompanying change in behavior. The sad truth is that there are millions of evangelicals who describe themselves as "born again" but whose faith is dead.

Consequently we have huge, active, wealthy mega-churches that are spiritually dead. Not only have these churches abandoned *orthodoxy* (straight thinking) for a syncretistic faith, they have abandoned *orthopraxy* (straight living) for a lifestyle that mimics the world. This causes the church to lose its credibility in a world that looks at

198

behavior when judging the legitimacy of a movement. The apostle Peter implores Christians, "Beloved, I beg you as sojourners and pilgrims, abstain from fleshy lusts which war against the soul, having your conduct honorable among the Gentiles, that when they speak against you as evildoers, they may, by your good works which they observe, glorify God in the day of visitation" (1 Peter 2:11-12).

Individual Ethics

Evangelicals need to recover personal ethics. We have been consumed with hot button issues like homosexuality and abortion, which take the focus off of our sins and onto others' sins. The practice of homosexuality is sin, but it is no more sinful than heterosexual immorality. The evangelical preoccupation with the issue of homosexuality is a way of drawing attention away from our own moral failings. There have been homosexuals in every congregation where I have served as pastor. They have always been "in the closet" and confided their struggles to me confidentially. I have clearly communicated to them the sinfulness of this behavior and the need to repent. I have stressed the grace of God and the forgiveness available to them. I have always found them willing to listen and seriously consider this offer.

In each of my churches there have been many heterosexual sinners. Sexual sin is rampant in evangelical Christianity. Adultery, fornication, "living together," pornography, and divorce are epidemic in evangelical churches. Seldom have I seen a genuine willingness to repent of these sins. This is the true sex scandal in the church. Mainline denominations are struggling over whether to allow unrepentant homosexuals in their congregations and in ordained ministry. The more urgent issue is what we do with unrepentant *heterosexuals* in our congregations!

The homosexuality issue is a diversionary tactic. Our self-righteous stance on this issue presents a face of evangelical righteousness to the culture, thereby drawing attention away from the persistent heterosexual sin in the church. In Jesus' words we "outwardly appear righteous to men, but inside you are full of hypocrisy and lawlessness" (Matthew 23:28). We are whitewashed tombs filled with filth, polished cups filled with self-indulgence (Matthew 23:25-27).

One of the evangelical arguments against gay marriage is that it will destroy the institution of marriage. The truth is that evangelicals have been dismantling the institution of marriage for decades. Divorce is more prevalent among Christians than non-Christians! We talk about "family values" while disrupting families by divorce. We take the Bible literally on homosexuality, while finding ingenious ways to reinterpret Jesus' clear teaching on divorce and remarriage. We do not need any help from the gay community in destroying marriage; we are doing a perfectly good job without them. The overwhelming need today is for an honest exposing of the sexual hypocrisy in the evangelical church.

We paint the moral issues of our society in terms of a "culture war" between Christians and an immoral secular culture. The truth is that we are fighting on the wrong front. In the Book of Joshua the city of Ai was taken by stealth. The warriors of Ai came out of the city and engaged the Hebrews on the battlefield. The Hebrews feigned defeat, fleeing before the men of Ai in order to lure them away from their city. Meanwhile, other Hebrew troops, who had been hiding behind Ai, entered the city unopposed and set it on fire. The soldiers of Ai looked behind them to see their homes going up in flames (Joshua 8:1-29). Evangelicals have gone into battle in the culture wars while our homes are in flames behind us. The main front in this spiritual war is not in the courts or the polling booths. It is in the homes and hearts of evangelicals.

The political agenda of the religious right is a misdirection of funds and energy. Their stands on the social issues are correct, but their strategy is wrong. They misunderstand the nature of the problem and therefore the nature of the solution. This is first and foremost a spiritual war. Political strategies will do little in such a battle. "For we do not wrestle against flesh and blood, but against principalities, against powers, against the rulers of the darkness of this age, against spiritual hosts of wickedness in the heavenly places" (Ephesians 6:12). The high places we should be most concerned with are not in Washington, but in the heavenly realms! The battle is engaged not in the courts, but on our knees! Our enemies are not gays, liberals, and evolutionists. Our enemies are "the rulers of the darkness of this age, against spiritual hosts of wickedness in the heavenly places" (Ephesians 6:12).

These enemies are experts in misdirection. They will do anything to get us to abandon our spiritual arsenal for worldly weapons. Their greatest ally is hypocrisy. Whether or not we win the battle for Washington, we will lose the war unless we redirect our resources. The scandal of evangelical immorality will not be solved by making American society more Christian. It will be solved by making American Christians more godly. Personal ethics need to regain center stage in evangelicalism. The evangelical preoccupation with political power and social influence needs to be replaced with a resurgence of spiritual influence and the power of the Holy Spirit.

Social Ethics

This does not mean that Christians should reenact the old fundamentalist retreat from the world and hide in the ghetto of moral individualism. The prophetic tradition of the Old Testament and the social themes of the preaching of Jesus will not allow that retreat. James was clear that saving faith included clothing the naked and feeding the hungry (James 2:15-16). Jesus said that the Final Judgment is based on the people's treatment of the hungry, homeless, poor, sick, and prisoners (Matthew 25:31-46). There is no competition between social ministry and personal morality. "Pure and undefiled religion before God and the Father is this: to visit orphans and widows in their trouble, and to keep oneself unspotted from the world" (James 1:27). Social ministry accompanies personal morality.

This is the role of Christian missions. Evangelicals have passively accepted the monopoly of government when it comes to solving social problems. Christ gave the church the responsibility to address these needs, and we have turned it over to the state. We moan that churches do not have the money to do such comprehensive social ministry, that only government can do it. This is untrue. American Christians are wealthy beyond the imagining of the rest of the world. The problem is not lack of money. A glance at the luxury of the megachurches and the lifestyles of middle-class Christians belies that idea. The problem is the materialism of evangelical Christians. We have bought into the life of consumerism. Megachurches grow by marketing to the American culture when they should be challenging it

There needs to be a resurgence of prophetic religion in American evangelical Christianity. There are a few voices in evangelicalism calling for this. Jim Wallis of *Sojourners* has articulated this for many years, most recently in his book *God's Politics*. Ronald Sider has been preaching it for decades, most notably in his book *Rich Christians in an Age of Hunger*. But both of these evangelicals leave me with the feeling that human government still is the solution. There seem to be postmillennial hopes hidden in these evangelical dreams.

The reality is that human government is the problem. Hunger, poverty and war are the products of worldly governments, and government will never solve the problems. We know how the story ends. Jesus said that the poor would always be with us.[26] The social problems of the globe will not be solved until Jesus returns. That does not remove the responsibility of ministering to those in need. But it does prevent us from fixing our hopes for a final solution of social ills by ascribing to governments the power that only rests with God.

The church is the body of Christ doing the work of Christ in the world. The problem is that the church is padding its pews while the world is going to hell. We suffer from obesity while our brothers and sisters starve. "But whoever has this world's goods, and sees his brother in need, and shuts up his heart against him, how does the love of God abide in him?" (1 John 3:17). There is a need to recover a sense of social responsibility to the least of these brothers. It begins not by lobbying politicians, but by preaching to Christians. It is financed not by taxes but tithes. Only 6 percent of evangelicals tithe. Imagine what could be done with the other 94 percent. The problem is not with the amount of money the United States gives to foreign aid. The problem lies with the amount of money Christians do not give to their churches. The problem is the materialistic values of Christians. We can prophesy to Washington all we want, but the solution remains in our own back pocket.

The Future of Evangelicalism

What does the future hold for evangelical Christianity? I am not hopeful. "Nevertheless, when the Son of Man comes, will He really find faith on the earth?" (Luke18:8). The failures of the megachurch movement reveal the worldliness of evangelical Christianity, and it is not getting any better. Evangelicalism will change, but I am not convinced it will change for the better.

The newest movement within evangelical Christianity is the *emergent church*, also called the *emerging church*. It is a protest movement dominated by Christians in their twenties who do not like the impersonality and showmanship of megachurch Christianity. Warren's Saddleback Church targets "baby-boomers," but boomer religion is already obsolete. The warehouse approach to religion does not attract the younger crowd. They cherish smaller, more informal, more intimate forms of Christianity.

The megachurch will pass away as boomers age, just as mainline churches have declined with the aging of the World War II generation. Even though megachurches try to be all things to all people, they have a negative image among the newest generation of Christians. To believers in their twenties, megachurches are large, impersonal, corporate entities. They are seen as the product of an older generation that shops at Wal-Mart and thinks that Disney World is a dream vacation. Just as liberal Protestant churches have declined in both attendance and influence, so the megachurch movement will also pass slowly into irrelevance in future decades.

What will take its place is not yet clear. The *emergent church* may blossom into a worldwide movement of grassroots Christianity echoing the house church movement of the early church. But it is showing signs of the same eclecticism, individualism, and doctrinal carelessness that characterize the megachurch movement. In reference to theology, one emergent church pastor states, "It's more important for us to feel like we're representing a beautiful expression of our life with God than it is to be right about everything."[27] Don Carson of Trinity Evangelical Divinity School is apprehensive about the theological recklessness of the new movement: "There is truth to be announced. If you start losing that, you really step outside what Christianity is."[28]

In any case, we need to take seriously the warnings of Scripture concerning religious movements in the end times. "Now the Spirit expressly says that in latter times some will depart from the faith, giving heed to deceiving spirits and doctrines of demons…" (1 Timothy 4:1). Before the coming of the Lord there will be a "falling away" (2 Thessalonians 2:3). There will be "unrighteous deception among those who perish, because they did not receive the love of the truth, that they may be saved. And for this reason God will sent them strong delusion, that they should believe the lie, that they all may be condemned who did not believe the truth but had pleasure in unrighteousness" (2 Thessalonians 2:10-12).

In combating those who are "deceiving and being deceived," Paul tells Timothy "But you must continue in the things which you have learned and been assured of, knowing from whom you have learned them, and that from childhood you have known the Holy Scriptures, which are able to make you wise for salvation through faith which is in Christ Jesus" (2 Timothy 3:13-15). In the face of compromises to the faith, we are to persevere, knowing that those who persevere to the end will be saved.[29] "Beware, brethren, lest there be in any of you an evil heart of unbelief in departing from the living God; but exhort one another daily, while it is called 'Today,' lest any of you be hardened through the deceitfulness of sin. For we have become partakers of Christ if we hold the beginning of our confidence steadfast to the end" (Hebrews 3:12-14).

ENDNOTES

Introduction

[1] Kristian M Bush, Kristen Alison Hall, Jennifer O Nettles, "Something More" from *Twice the Speed of Life* performed by Sugarland (Nashville, TN: Mercury Records, released October 26, 2004).

[2] Rick Warren, *The Purpose-Driven Church* (Grand Rapids: Zondervan, 1995), 14.

[3] George Mair, A *Life With a Purpose* (New York: Berkley Books, 2005), 157.

[4] Purpose-Driven Website, *Ken Camp,* "Second Reformation' will unify church, Warren tells Dallas GDOP," www.purposedriven.com/en-US/AboutUs/PDinthe-News/Second_Reformation_will_unify_church.htm (accessed June 1, 2005).

[5] John MacArthur, *Reckless Faith* (Wheaton IL: Crossway Books, 1994), 28-29.

[6] Chris Accardy, "Neo-Liberalism: The Liberal Ethos in Rick Warren's *The Purpose-Driven Church*," *Reformation & Revival* (Summer 1998), Volume 7.

[7] John MacArthur, *Ashamed of the Gospel* (Wheaton IL: Crossway Books, 1993), 23.

[8] Warren, *The Purpose-Driven Life* (Grand Rapids: Zondervan, 2002), 146.

[9] Mair, *A Life With a Purpose*, 126.

[10] Warren, *The Purpose-Driven Church*, 199.

Chapter 1 - It's Not About You...Or Is It?

[1] Rick Warren, *The Purpose-Driven Life* (Grand Rapids: Zondervan, 2002), 17.

[2] Ibid., 18-19.

[3] Ibid., 5 (unnumbered).

[4] Warren, *The Purpose-Driven Life*, 9.

[5] Michael Denton quoted in Warren, *The Purpose-Driven Life*, 24.

[6] Russell Kelfer, quoted in Warren, *The Purpose-Driven Life*, 25.

[7] Warren, *The Purpose-Driven Life*, 136. Italics in the original.

[8] Ibid., 30-33.

[9] Ibid., 173.

[10] George Barna, *The Second Coming of the Church* (Nashville: Word Publishing, 1998), 20.

[11] Rick Warren, *The Purpose-Driven Church* (Grand Rapids: Zondervan, 1995), 27.

[12] Warren, *The Purpose-Driven Church*, 33.

[13] Ibid., 19.

[14] Ibid., 25.

[15] Ibid., 26.

[16] Warren, *The Purpose-Driven Life*, 287-8.

[17] Warren, *The Purpose-Driven Church*, 29.

[18] Ibid., 30.

[19] Ibid., 169-172.

[20] George Mair, A *Life With a Purpose* (New York: Berkley Books, 2005), 73.

[21] *USA Today*, Rick Warren interview: This evangelist has a 'Purpose.' July 21, 2003, D1.

[22] Dave Hunt and James White, *Debating Calvinism* (Sisters, OR; Multnomah, 2004), 124.

[23] Mair, A *Life With a Purpose*, 93.

[24] Ibid., 93-4.

[25] Ibid., 96.

[26] Warren, *The Purpose-Driven Life*, 182.

[27] Mair, A *Life With a Purpose*, 100.

[28] Ibid., 105.

[29] Ibid., 108.

[30] Hour of Power, Robert Schuller, Program # 1783, "What Will be the Future of This Ministry?" April 4, 2004, quoted in Warren Smith, Deceived on Purpose, 103.

[31] Tim Stafford, "A Regular Purpose-Driven Guy,' *Christianity Today*, November 8, 2002, Volume 46, No. 12, accessed at www.christianitytoday.com/ct/2002/012/1.42.html.

[32] Warren, *The Purpose-Driven Life*, 181.

[33] Robert Schuller, *Self Esteem: the New Reformation* (Waco, Texas: Word Books, 1982) 120.

[34] Richard Abanes, *Rick Warren and the Purpose that Drives Him* (Eugene, OR: Harvest house Publishers, 2005), 99-106.

[35] Warren, *The Purpose-Driven Life*, 247.

[36] Ibid., 63.

[37] Ibid., 275.

[38] Ibid., 247.

[39] Ibid., 213.

[40] Ibid., 104.

[41] Warren, *The Purpose-Driven Church*, 243.

[42] Ibid., 219.

[43] Ibid., 220.

[44] Ibid., 221.

[45] Ibid., 227.

[46] Ibid., 229.

[47] Jeff Robinson, "Sproul: Reformation & revival built upon power of the Gospel," Baptist Press; June 29, 2005. www.bpnews.net/bpnews.asp?ID=21118, accessed June 29, 2005.

[48] Ibid.

[49] Warren, *The Purpose-Driven Church*, 238.

[50] Ibid., 295.

[51] Warren, *The Purpose-Driven Life*, 237-9, 251.

[52] Warren, *The Purpose-Driven Life*, 12.

[53] Ibid., 261.

[54] Ibid., 136-7.

[55] Ibid., 179. Italics in original.

[56] Ibid., 180.

[57] Warren, *The Purpose-Driven Church*, 81.

[58] Warren, *The Purpose-Driven Life*, 20.

[59] Ibid., 41-42. Italics in original.

[60] Ibid., 41.

[61] Ibid., 42.

[62] Ibid., 42.

[63] "Drive," Etext of *Webster's Unabridged Dictionary** Copyright © 1996 by MICRA, Inc. Plainfield, N.J. www.everything2.com/index.pl?node=Drive accessed July 6, 2005.

[64] These 42 occurrences in the *New International Version* translate seven different Greek words.

[65] 27 times.

[66] 1 John 4:18.

[67] 2 Corinthians 12:11.

[68] John 6:37.

[69] There are 162 occurrences of the English words "drive," "driven," or "drove" in the NIV Old Testament. These translate 22 different Hebrew words.

[70] 76 times.

[71] 21 times.

[72] Judges 4:21.

[73] Ahmed Abdulwahab, "Religious Roundtable" on *Speakeasy Radio with Bob Henry*. WBVP, 1230 AM, Beaver Falls, Pennsylvania, 2003.

[74] Warren, *The Purpose-Driven Life*, 227-280, Purpose # 4.

[75] Ibid., 77.

[76] Ibid., 78.

[77] Ibid., 80.

[78] Ibid., 81.

[79] Ibid., 83.

[80] Ibid.

[81] Ibid., 84.

[82] Warren, *The Purpose-Driven Life*, 18.

[83] Udo W. Middelmann, *The Market-Driven Church* (Wheaton IL: Crossway Books, 2004), 49-67.

Chapter 2 - Doctrine for Dummies

[1] Warren Smith, *Deceived On Purpose: The New Age Implications of the Purpose-Driven Church*, Second Edition (Magalia, CA: Mountain Stream Press, 2004), 8.

[2] Richard Abanes, *Rick Warren and the Purpose that Drives Him* (Eugene, OR: Harvest house Publishers, 2005), 127.

[3] Rick Warren, *The Purpose-Driven Church* (Grand Rapids: Zondervan, 1995), 53.

[4] Ibid.

[5] Warren, *The Purpose-Driven Church*, 300.

[6] Rick Warren, *The Purpose-Driven Life* (Grand Rapids: Zondervan, 2002), 186.

[7] Ibid., 183.

[8] Ibid., 72.

[9] Ibid., 34.

[10] Ibid., 124.

[11] Os Guinness, *Dining With the Devil: The Megachurch Movement Flirts With Modernity* (Grand Rapids: Baker Books, 1993) 84.

[12] Warren, *The Purpose-Driven Church*, 228.

[13] Ibid., 290.

[14] Ibid., 226.

[15] George Mair, *A Life With a Purpose* (New York: Berkley Books, 2005), 23.

[16] Warren, *The Purpose-Driven Life*, 161.

[17] Ibid., 162.

[18] John Winston Lennon, Paul McCartney "All You Need is Love" from *Yellow Submarine* (Capitol Records, 1969).

[19] Saddleback Church website, "What We Believe," www.saddleback.com/flash/believe.html (accessed June 13, 2005).

[20] Douglas D. Webster, *Selling Jesus: What's Wrong with Marketing the Church?* (Downer's Grove, IL: Intervarsity, 1992), 84.

[21] Warren, *The Purpose-Driven Life*, 161.

[22] Nathan Busenitz, "*The Purpose-Driven Life*: A Review" (Pulpit Shepherds Fellowship, Copyright 2003) www.biblebb.com/files/pdl.htm (accessed May 28, 2005).

[23] Saddleback Church, "What We Believe," www.saddleback.com/flash/believe2.html (accessed May 28, 2005).

[24] Warren, *The Purpose-Driven Church*, 199.

[25] "The Baptist Faith and Message," II. *God*, www.sbc.net/bfm/bfm2000.asp (accessed June 25, 2005).

[26] Saddleback Church, "What We Believe," *Who is God?* www.saddleback.com/flash/believe2.html (accessed June 25, 2005).

27 Guinness, *Dining With the Devil,* 84.

28 Warren, *The Purpose-Driven Church,* 102.

29 Warren, *The Purpose-Driven Life,* 101.

30 Warren, *The Purpose-Driven Church,* 299.

31 Ibid., 58.

32 Saddleback Church, "What We Believe," *Who is Jesus?* www.saddleback.com/flash/believe2.html (accessed June 25, 2005).

33 Chris Accardy, "Neo-Liberalism: The Liberal Ethos in Rick Warren's *The Purpose-Driven Church" Reformation & Revival* (Summer 1998), Volume 7, 97.

34 Warren, *The Purpose-Driven Life,* 112.

35 Ibid., 86.

36Ibid., 9.

37 Ibid., 58.

38 Ibid., 58.

39 Ibid., 58-9.

40 John MacArthur, *Hard To Believe* (Nashville: Thomas Nelson Publishers, 2003), 12.

41 H. Richard Niebuhr quoted in Guiness, *Dining With the Devil,* 78.

42 Warren, *The Purpose-Driven Life,* 59.

43 Ibid., 101.

44 *Ibid.,* 171-2.

45 Saddleback Church website, "What We Believe," *What is Salvation?*

46 Warren, *The Purpose-Driven Life,* 175.

47 Ibid., 37.

48Ibid., 174.

49 Ibid., 180.

50 Warren, *The Purpose-Driven Church,* 15.

51 Mair, *A Life With a Purpose,* 18.

52 Joe Fisher, "A Critique of The *Purpose-Driven Life* by Rick Warren," www.consensuslutheran.org/modules.

php?file=articles&name=News&op=modload&sid=32
3 (accessed June 19, 2005).

53 "Americans' Bible Knowledge Is In the Ballpark, But Often Off Base," *The Barna Update*, July 12, 2000, The Barna Group , www.barna.org/FlexPage.aspx?Page=BarnaUpdate&BarnaUpdateID=66 (accessed November 23, 2005).

54 Warren, *The Purpose-Driven Life*, 58.

55 Ibid., 175 (quoting the CEV translation of Ephesians 4:23).

56 Ibid., 187-8.

57 Ibid., 174-5.

58 The Barna Update, *Four Out of Ten Adults Discuss Religious Matters During the Week*, June 9, 2003, www.barna.org/FlexPage.aspx?Page=BarnaUpdate&BarnaUpdateID=140.

59 David Wells, *No Place For Truth: Whatever Happened to Evangelical Theology?* (Grand Rapids, MI: Wm. B. Eerdmans, 1993).

Chapter 3–The Market-Driven Life

1 Rich Karlgaard, "Purpose-Driven," Forbes.com: www.forbes.com/business/forbes/2004/0216/039.html (February 16, 2004).

2 Luisa Kroll, "Christian Capitalism: Megachurches, Megabusinesses" Forbes.com: www.forbes.com/2003/09/17/cz_lk_0917megachurch.html (September 17, 2003).

3 James B. Twitchell, *Branded Nation* (New York: Simon & Schuster, 2004), 82-3.

4 George Mair, A *Life With a Purpose* (New York: Berkley Books, 2005), 125.

5 Twitchell, *Branded Nation*, 81.

6 Ibid.

[7] Kurt Gebhards, "Choking on Choices: Combating Consumerism With a Biblical Mindset," in *Fool's Gold: Discerning Truth in An Age of Error* (Wheaton, IL: Crossway Books, 2005) John MacArthur, General Editor, 164.

[8] Mair, A *Life With a Purpose*, 125.

[9] Gebhards, "Choking on Choices," 164.

[10] Ibid., 172.

[11] Twitchell, *Branded Nation*, 56.

[12] Rick Warren, *The Purpose-Driven Church* (Grand Rapids: Zondervan, 1995), 54.

[13] Warren, *The Purpose-Driven Church*, 220.

[14] Ibid., 220-221.

[15] James B. Twitchell, *Branded Nation* (New York: Simon & Schuster, 2004), 66-67.

[16] Warren, *The Purpose-Driven Church*, 45.

[17] Alan Wolfe, *The Transformation of American Religion* (New York: Free Press, 2003), 113.

[18] Norman Geisler & Ronald M. Brooks, *Let Us Reason* (Grand Rapids: Baker Book House, 1990), 103.

[19] Rick Warren, *The Purpose-Driven Life* (Grand Rapids: Zondervan, 2002), 285.

[20] Donald McGavran, "For Such a Time As This" (unpublished address, 1970) cited in *God, Man and Church Growth* (Grand Rapids, MI: Eerdmans, 1973), A. R. Tipper, ed., 147.

[21] Warren, *The Purpose-Driven Church*, 15.

[22] C. Peter Wagner, *Your Church Can Grow* (Ventura, CA: Regal Books, 1976) 160-161.

[23] Warren, *The Purpose-Driven Life*, 38.

[24] Nathan Busenitz, Á Sense of Purpose: Evaluating the Claims of *The Purpose-Driven Life*" in *Fool's Gold? Discerning Truth in an Age of Error* John MacArthur, General Editor (Wheaton IL: Crossway Books, 2005), 59.

[25] MacArthur, *Ashamed of the Gospel*, xiii.

26 Warren, *The Purpose-Driven Life,* 9.

27 Norman L. Geisler & Ronald M. Brooks, *Come, Let Us Reason Together* (Grand Rapids, MI: Baker Book House, 1990), 103.

28 Laura Penny, *Your Call Is Important to Us: The Truth about Bull----* (Crown, 2005) quoted in *USA Today,* July 28, 2005, 5D.

29 Kirk Cameron and Ray Comfort, *The Way of the Master* (Wheaton, IL: Tyndale House Publishers, 2004), 54.

30 Bob DeWaay, "The Gospel: A Method or a Message? How *The Purpose-Driven Life* Obscures the Gospel," *Critical Issues Commentary* (January/February 2004), Issue 80, www.twincityfellowship.com/cic/articles/issue80.htm (accessed March 8, 2004).

31 "Pragmatism: Archenemy of Theology," www.geocities.com/hebrews928/1hope.html (accessed August 2, 2005).

32 "Hour of Power" broadcast July 23, 2005.

33 Warren, *The Purpose-Driven Church,* 221.

34 Ibid., 259.

35 Ibid., 262.

36 Middelmann, *The Market-Driven Church,* 54.

37 MacArthur, *Ashamed of the Gospel,* 192.

38 "Notes," *The Sword and the Trowel* (October 1888 and January 1889) quoted in John MacArthur, *Ashamed of the Gospel,* 192.

Chapter 4 - Gimme That Showtime Religion

1 Udo W. Middelmann, *The Market-Driven Church* (Wheaton IL: Crossway Books, 2004), 124.

2 Neil Postman, *Amusing Ourselves to Death: Public Discourse in the Age of Show Business* (New York: Penguin Books, 1985), 3.

3 Middelmann, *The Market-Driven Church,* 124.

[4] Ibid., 53.

[5] Alan Wolfe, *The Transformation of American Religion* (New York: Free Press, 2003), 212.

[6] Rick Warren, *The Purpose-Driven Church* (Grand Rapids: Zondervan, 1995), 41.

[7] Rick Warren, *The Purpose-Driven Life* (Grand Rapids: Zondervan, 2002), 64.

[8] Warren, *The Purpose-Driven Church,* 207-308.

[9] Warren, *The Purpose-Driven Life,* 64.

[10] Ibid, 65.

[11] Ibid.

[12] Ibid, 67.

[13] Ibid.

[14] Ibid., 74.

[15] Ibid., 75.

[16] Warren, *The Purpose-Driven Church,* 231.

[17] Warren, *The Purpose-Driven Church,* 220.

[18] Ibid., 42.

[19] Ibid., 256.

[20] Warren, *The Purpose-Driven Church,* 279.

[21] Ibid., 285.

[22] Ibid.

[23] Quoted in Wolfe, *The Transformation of American Religion,* 29.

[24] Ibid.

[25] Warren, *The Purpose-Driven Church,* 281.

[26] Udo W. Middelmann, *The Market-Driven Church* (Wheaton, IL: Crossway Books, 2004), 145.

[27] Rick Warren interview, "Myths of the Modern Mega-Church," *The Pew Forum's Biannual Faith Angle Conference* (May 23, 2005, Key West, Florida), The Pew Forum on Religion & Public Life, pewforum.org/events/index. php?EventID=80 (accessed August 23, 2005).

[28] Ibid.

[29] Os Guinness, *Dining With the Devil* (Grand Rapids, MI: Baker Books, 1993), 79-80.

[30] Middelmann, *The Market-Driven Church*, 139.

[31] Warren, *The Purpose-Driven Church*, 259.

[32] Ibid., 273.

[33] Warren, *The Purpose-Driven Life*, 79.

[34] Ibid., 85.

[35] Warren, *The Purpose-Driven Church*, 240.

[36] Ibid., 289.

[37] Linda Louise McCartney, Paul McCartney, "Silly Love Songs" performed by Paul McCartney And Wings, from *Wings At The Speed Of Sound* album (EMI International, 1993).

[38] Warren, *The Purpose-Driven Church*, 256.

[39] Warren, *The Purpose-Driven Life*, 183.

[40] Warren, *The Purpose-Driven Church*, 284-5.

[41] Warren, *The Purpose-Driven Life*, 102.

[42] Ibid., 103.

[43] Huston Smith, *The World's Religions* (New York: Harper Collins, 1991), 26.

[44] Warren, *The Purpose-Driven Life*, 103.

[45] Warren, *The Purpose-Driven Church*, 290.

[46] Saddleback Church website, "What We Believe," www.saddleback.com/flash/believe.html accessed June 13, 2005.

[47] Warren, *The Purpose-Driven Church*, 227.

[48] Ibid., 226.

Chapter 5–Spiritual But Not Religious

[1] Rick Warren, *The Purpose-Driven Church* (Grand Rapids: Zondervan, 1995), 171.

[2] Ibid., 41.

[3] Ibid., 238.

[4] Ibid., 198.

[5] Ibid., 229-230.

[6] Rick Warren, *The Purpose-Driven Life* (Grand Rapids: Zondervan, 2002), 183.

[7] Alan Wolfe, *The Transformation of American Religion* (New York: Free Press, 2003), 182-183.

[8] "Rick Warren interview: This evangelist has a 'Purpose.'" *USA Today* (July 21, 2003), D1.

[9] Email dated February 26, 2004 on www.challies.com/archives/000124.html (accessed 9/30/04).

[10] 2 Timothy 2:17.

[11] Douglas R. Groothuis, *Unmasking the New Age* (Downer's Grove, IL: Intervarsity Press), 18-31.

[12] Ibid., 18.

[13] Ibid., 20.

[14] Paul Yonggi Cho, *The Fourth Dimension: The Key to Putting Your Faith to Work For a Successful Life,* Foreword by Robert Schuller (S. Plainfield, NJ: Bridge Publishing, Inc., 1979), 44.

[15] "Rick Warren interview: This Evangelist Has a 'Purpose.'" *USA Today* (July 21, 2003), D1.

[16] *Denison Magazine,* (Summer 2005), 35.

[17] "What We Believe," *Saddleback Church website,* www.saddleback.com/flash/believe.html (accessed June 13, 2005).

[18] Ibid.

[19] Warren Smith, *Deceived On Purpose: The New Age Implications of the Purpose-Driven Church,* Second Edition (Magalia, CA: Mountain Stream Press, 2004).

[20] Groothuis, *Unmasking the New Age,* 15.

[21] George Mair, *A Life With a Purpose* (New York: Berkley Books, 2005), 93.

[22] Smith, *Deceived On Purpose,* 103.

[23] Ibid., 112-113.

24 Bernie Siegel, *Love, Medicine & Miracles* (New York: Harper-Collins Publishers, 1998) 18, quoted in Warren Smith, *Deceived On Purpose*, 47-48.

25 Robert H. Schuller, *Prayer: My Soul's Adventure With God: A Spiritual Autobiography* (Nashville, TN: Thomas Nelson, 1995), unnumbered opening page.

26 Warren, *The Purpose-Driven Life*, 31.

27 Neale Donald Walsch, *The New Revelations: A Conversation with God* (New York: Atria Books, 2002), 281.

28 Neale Donald Walsch, *Conversations With God: an uncommon dialogue, Book 2* (Charlottesville, VA Hampton Road Publishing Company, 1997), 1.

29 Warren, *The Purpose-Driven Life*, Dedication page.

30 "Welcome to the P.E.A.C.E. Plan" (www.saddlebackfamily.com/peace) accessed August 8, 2005.

31 Ibid.

32 Smith, *Deceived On Purpose*, 137. Bold type in original.

33 Richard Abanes, *Rick Warren and the Purpose that Drives Him* (Eugene, OR: Harvest house Publishers, 2005), 23.

34 Ibid., 13-14.

35 Beliefnet Editors, *From the Ashes: A Spiritual Response to the Attack on America* (USA: Rodale Inc., 2001).

36 Smith, *Deceived On Purpose*, 139-140.

37 *Living Your Purpose in Today's Turbulent World*, www.cwg.org/index2.html (accessed August 10, 2005).

38 Smith, *Deceived On Purpose*, 8.

39 Ibid.

40 Warren, *The Purpose-Driven Life*, 88.

41 Robert H. Schuller, *Hour of Power*, Program 1762, "God's Word: Rebuild, Renew, Restore," November 9, 2003, www.hourofpower.org/booklets/bookletdetail.cfm?ArticleID=2107), 5.

[42] Bernie Siegel, *Prescriptions for Living* (New York: HarperCollins Publishers, 1999), 107.

[43] *Messages from Maitreya the Christ*, quoted in Smith, *Deceived On Purpose*, 84-85.

[44] Warren, *The Purpose-Driven Life*, 79. Italics in original.

[45] Ibid., 172. Italics in original.

[46] Richard Abanes, *Rick Warren and the Purpose that Drives Him,* 95-96.

[47] Ibid., 90.

[48] Ibid., 89.

[49] "TM Program and Transcendental Consciousness" (www.tm.org/discover/glance/index.html), accessed August 8, 2005.

[50] Warren, *Purpose-Driven Life*, 235.

[51] Ibid., 237.

[52] Smith, *Deceived on Purpose,* 111.

[53] Warren, *The Purpose-Driven Life,* 238.

[54] Ibid., 17.

[55] Bertrand Russell, *Why I am Not a Christian,* lecture delivered on March 6, 1927, www.users.drew.edu/~jlenz/whynot.html (accessed August 10, 2005).

[56] Warren, *The Purpose-Driven Life,* 41.

[57] Ibid., 33.

[58] Ibid., 248.

Chapter 6–Recovering the Evangelical Essentials

[1] David F. Wells, *No Place For Truth Or Whatever Happened to Evangelical Theology* (Grand Rapids, MI: William B. Eerdmans Publishing Company: 1993), 95.

[2] Rick Warren, *The Purpose-Driven Life* (Grand Rapids: Zondervan, 2002), 287-8.

[3] Kirk Cameron and Ray Comfort, *The Way of the Master* Wheaton, IL: Tyndale House Publishers, 2004), 53.

[4] Bill Bright, *The Coming Revival* (Orlando, FL: New Life Publications, 1995), 63.

[5] George Barna, *The Second Coming of the Church* (Nashville, TH: Word Publishing, 1998), 5.

[6] Mark Noll, *The Scandal of the Evangelical Mind* (Grand Rapids, MI: William B. Eerdmans Publishing Company, 1994), 3.

[7] Wells, *No Place For Truth*, 112-113.

[8] Ronald J. Sider, *The Scandal of the Evangelical Conscience* (Grand Rapids, MI: Baker Books, 2005), 90-91.

[9] *The Cambridge Declaration* of the Alliance of Confessing Evangelicals, www.reformed.org/documents/cambridge.html (accessed August 26, 2005).

[10] A good collection is *Baptist Confessions, Covenants, and Catechisms*, Timothy and Denise George, editors (Nashville, TN: Broadman & Holman Publishers, 1996).

[11] Sider, *The Scandal of the Evangelical Conscience*, 116.

[12] Warren, *The Purpose-Driven Life*, 121.

[13] Rick Warren, *The Purpose-Driven Church* (Grand Rapids: Zondervan, 1995), 355. Italics added.

[14] Alan Wolfe, *The Transformation of American Religion* (New York: Free Press, 2003), 112.

[15] Kimon Howland Sargeant, *Seeker Churches: Promoting Traditional Religion in a Nontraditional Way* (New Brunswick, NJ: Rutgers University Press, 2000), 663.

[16] Sider, *The Scandal of the Evangelical Conscience*, 57-58.

[17] Wolfe, *The Transformation of American Religion*, 116-117.

[18] Barna, *The Second Coming of the Church*, 19.

[19] Peter Gillquist, *Why We Haven't Changed the World* (Old Tappan, NJ: Revell, 1982), 56-57.

[20] Haddon Robinson quoted in Sider, *The Scandal of the Evangelical Conscience*, 115.

[21] Marlin Jeschke, "How Discipline Died," *Christianity Today* (August 2005), 31.

[22] Wolfe, *The Transformation of American Religion*, 44.

[23] 1 Peter 2:17.

[24] Warren, *The Purpose-Driven Church,* 287.

[25] Michael Horton quoted in Sider, *The Scandal of the Evangelical Conscience*, 15.

[26] Matthew 26:11.

[27] Doug Pagitt, pastor, Solomon's Porch Church, interviewed in "The Emerging Church, Part One," *Religion & Ethics Newsweekly* (July 8, 2005 Episode no. 845) www.pbs.org/wnet/religionandethics/week845/cover.html.

[28] Don Carson quoted in "The Emerging Church, Part One," *Religion & Ethics Newsweekly.*

[29] Matthew 24:13.